# 2000 MOST COMMON
# DUTCH WORDS
# IN CONTEXT

Get Fluent & Increase Your Dutch
Vocabulary with 2000 Dutch Phrases

**Dutch Language Lessons**

# Free Book Reveals The 6 Step Blueprint That Took Students **From Language Learners To Fluent In 3 Months**

- **6 Unbelievable Hacks** that will accelerate your learning curve

- **Mind Training:** why memorizing vocabulary is easy

- **One Hack To Rule Them All:** This secret nugget will blow you away...

Head over to **LingoMastery.com/hacks**
and claim your free book now!

# Introduction

Congratulations! If you're reading this, it means you've just taken the first step towards mastering the Dutch language! Dutch is spoken by 17 million people in The Netherlands, 6.5 million people in Belgium, and approximately another million people living around the world. Whether you're living in The Netherlands or Belgium right now, moving there soon, or just want to learn the language to speak to your Dutch-speaking friends and family: this phrasebook is an excellent tool for beginners, as well as intermediate learners, to support their language learning journey.

A lot of research has been carried out about foreign language acquisition over the last decades, and we've based this method on aspects that most academic studies agree on:

- Vocabulary is the foundation to learning a foreign language. Being able to recognize words in the language you're learning, both written and spoken, is the basis of eventually mastering the language, even if you don't understand the grammar constructions being used in the sentence. In order to understand a lot of the language quickly, it's pertinent to focus on the most frequently used words, which is the most effective way to progress quickly. To illustrate this, studies have found that learning the top two thousand most frequently used words will help you understand 84% of non-fiction reading material, 86.1% of fiction reading material, and 92.7% of oral speech.

- Context is key. It has been proven that humans can retain new language best when it is presented within a context, which is exactly what the phrases we've designed for you are doing: providing a context. We've chosen to include a range of possible situations, as well as sentences in the affirmative, negative and questions, in order to expose you

1

to vocabulary used in a variety of circumstances.

- It's important to use the four best skills needed when acquiring a second language: listening, reading, speaking and writing. This book and its accompanying audio recordings focus on helping you use the first two skills, creating an excellent foundation for when you're ready to move on to the speaking and writing stage.

- Self-study methods have to be practical in order to work, which is why the combination of audio recordings and the written script are so effective, since you can easily fit them into your daily activities by listening to the recordings when you're in the car, cooking, on the train, or even at the gym!

Although we'd love to begin the book right away by helping you learn the vocabulary we've provided, here are a few tips and recommendations for you to get the most out of this book.

**Recommendations for readers of 2000 Most Common Words in Dutch:**

- For self-study, it's very helpful to set specific and achievable goals for yourself to ensure you stay on track. For example, you could decide to focus on 50 phrases a week, listening to them several times and writing them out on paper too. That way, you'll have mastered all of the vocabulary within less than 10 months by studying only 1-2 hours a week!

- It's also very useful to team up with someone who already speaks Dutch or is also learning Dutch, so you can help keep each other on track while practicing together.

- Some people find pronouncing Dutch quite hard, so make sure to say the phrases out loud to get your brain and tongue used to the pronunciation. We promise there is some logic behind it!

- Another very beneficial activity is to write the phrases you're studying on pieces of paper, which will help you remember the words and their meanings and can be used as excellent study tools. You could cut the phrases in half and make a matching exercise - read only the first few words and see if you remember the rest; keep collecting them as a way to go back to phrases learned a while ago - the possibilities are endless.

- Since context is so important, another tip is to take each phrase, change a few words so they match your reality more closely and write out this new, personalized phrase in a notebook.

- In translation of words you may note that some words are separated by ',' and others are separated by ';'. Be attentive: the former one is for synonyms and the latter one is for completely different words.

Also, here's a list of abbreviations used in the book to classify the parts of speech of the word definitions:

[n] - noun

[v] - verb

[adj] - adjective

[adv] - adverb

[art] - article

[conj] - conjunction

[interj] - interjection

[num] - number

[poss] - possessive

[prep] - preposition

[pron] - pronoun

[~]- translation not an exact equivalent

A Few Grammar Notes

In many ways, the Dutch language is fairly closely related to the English language, especially in terms of vocabulary.

3

Even though we're not delving into the daunting world of verb tenses and conjugation here, it's worth mentioning that verb conjugations in Dutch aren't all that complex, although some verbs are irregular. What people learning the Dutch language tend to find most difficult is the order of words. In simple affirmative tenses, the word order follows the subject-verb-object (SVO) order that is used in English and the majority of other languages (i.e.: I have a car, would be *Ik heb een auto*), but it becomes more complicated in questions, perfect tenses and with prepositional verbs. We've included many phrases in the negative and question forms to show you how they affect sentence order and help you recognize and master them. The good thing is that your brain will also intuitively start to recognize patterns from the phrases without having to go through pages and pages of grammar explanations!

In order to help you understand Dutch verbs and their conjugation a little, we've included whether the verb is conjugated in the:

- 1$^{st}$, 2$^{nd*}$ or 3$^{rd}$ person (this always refers to singular), or all singular/plural subjects.

- Present, past, future or conditional tense

Here's an example of the conjugation of the verb *lopen* (to walk) in the present tense:

|  | **Singular** |  | **Plural** |  |
|---|---|---|---|---|
| 1st person | Ik loop | *I walk* | We/wij lopen | *We walk* |
| 2nd person | Je/jij loopt | *You walk* | Jullie lopen | *You walk* |
| 3rd person | Hij, ze/zij, u** loopt | *He, she walks, you walk* | Ze/zij lopen | *They walk* |

*Please note: whenever it says (1st and 2nd person - present tense), this means that the verb is only in that form for 2nd person when it's a question.

**U is a formal way of addressing "you", which is always conjugated in the singular but is, in fact, used to address either one person or a group of people.

Without any further ado, it's time to set sail and start your Dutch language journey today, no life jacket needed: if you feel the waves of words are getting too rough, just take a break and come back aboard a few hours or days later!

## Let's get started!

# THE 2000 MOST COMMON
# DUTCH WORDS IN CONTEXT

### 1- de [art] *the*

De zon schijnt vandaag.
The sun is shining today.

### 2 - en [conj] *and*

Ik heb een kat en een hond.
I have a cat and a dog.

### 3 - van [prep] *from, of*

Van mijn huis naar Theo's huis is drie kwartier fietsen.
From my house to Theo's house, it takes three-quarters of an hour by bike.

### 4 - het [art, pron] *the; it*

Is dat het Van Gogh Museum?
Is that the Van Gogh Museum?

### 5 - een [art] *a, an*

Kijk, er zit een grote vogel in de boom!
Look, there's a big bird in the tree!

### 6 - in [prep] *in*

Haar sleutels zitten niet in haar tas.
Her keys aren't in her bag.

### 7 - is [v] *is (3<sup>rd</sup> person singular in the present tense)*

Die mevrouw met het rode haar is een bekend schrijfster.
That lady with the red hair is a well-known author.

### 8 - op [prep, adj] *on, at; finished*

Je mag de kleren gewoon **op** bed leggen.
You may just put the clothes **on** the bed.

### 9 - te [adv, prep] *too; in, by, to*

Denk je dat deze broek **te** klein is voor mij?
Do you think these pants are **too** small for me?

### 10 - met [prep] *with*

Ik zou graag een keer naar India willen gaan **met** mijn familie.
I would like to go to India **with** my family one day.

### 11 - voor [adv, prep] *before; for, in front of*

**Voor** het huis is een tuin met bomen en struiken.
**In front of** the house is a garden with trees and bushes.

### 12 - dat [conj, pron] *that*

De lerares vindt **dat** filmpje perfect voor haar leerlingen.
The teacher thinks **that** video is perfect for her students.

### 13 - je [pron, poss] *you; your*

Heb **je** gevraagd of **je** ouders hulp nodig hebben?
Did **you** ask if **your** parents need help?

### 14 - zijn [poss, v] *his; to be (plural subjects – present tense)*

Mijn zus en ik **zijn** wel een beetje jaloers op jullie grote tuin.
My sister and I **are** a little jealous of your big garden.

### 15 - die [pron] *those; that*

Mogen wij **die** klompen in maat 40 proberen, alstublieft?

Can we try **those** clogs in a size 40, please?

### 16 - ik [pron] *I*

**Ik** ben nog niet naar het nieuwe museum geweest.
**I** haven't been to the new museum yet.

### 17 - aan [prep] *on; to*

De schilderijen van Rembrandt hangen **aan** de muur.
The paintings by Rembrandt are hanging **on** the wall.

### 18 - niet [n, adv] *staple; not; no*

We hebben ons huiswerk voor Nederlands nog **niet** af.
We have **not** finished our Dutch homework yet.

### 19 - om [prep, conj] *at; to*

Denk je dat ze hier precies **om** 8 uur zullen zijn?
Do you think they'll be here **at** 8 o'clock sharp?

### 20 - ook [adv] *also, too*

Ongeveer 60% van de Belgen spreekt **ook** Nederlands.
About 60% of Belgians **also** speak Dutch.

### 21 - er [adv] *there*

**Er** waren zoveel mensen in de stad dat ik nergens kon parkeren.
**There** were so many people in town that I couldn't park anywhere.

### 22 - als [conj] *if, like, as; when*

**Als** je niet opschiet, kom je te laat!
**If** you don't hurry up, you'll be late!

**23 - of** [conj] *or*

Hebben jullie liever thee **of** koffie bij het gebak?
Do you prefer tea **or** coffee with your pastry?

**24 - bij** [prep, n] *close to, with; bee*

De toeristen staan **bij** het monument foto's te maken.
The tourists are standing **close to** the monument taking photos.

**25 - maar** [conj, adv] *but; only*

We waren erg moe, **maar** we hebben toch van het feestje genoten.
We were very tired, **but** we still enjoyed the party.

**26 - u** [pron] *you (formal, singular and plural)*

Heeft **u** eventueel nog verdere vragen?
Do **you** happen to have any further questions?

**27 - door** [prep] *through; due to; by*

Het water lekte **door** het dak.
The water leaked **through** the roof.

**28 - deze** [pron] *this, these*

Ik wil de muren in **deze** kamer volgend jaar verven.
I want to paint the walls in **this** room next year.

**29 - dan** [adv] *then; than*

Mijn zus wil eerst genoeg sparen en **dan** een huis kopen.
My sister wants to save enough money first, and **then** buy a house.

**30 - we** [pron] *we*

**We** zien onze familie niet vaak genoeg.

**We** don't see our family often enough.

### 31 - dit [pron] *this*

Heeft u ooit eerder in **dit** restaurant gegeten?
Have you ever eaten in **this** restaurant before?

### 32 - worden [v] *to become; to get + adjective (infinitive and plural subjects in the present tense; also used as the auxiliary verb for perfect tenses)*

Mijn grootouders **worden** moe als ze te lang moeten lopen.
My grandparents **get** tired when they have to walk for too long.

### 33 - naar [adj, adv] *to, towards; unpleasant*

Pardon, gaat deze trein **naar** Utrecht?
Excuse me, does this train go **to** Utrecht?

### 34 - uit [prep, adj, v] *from, out of; off; to express yourself (singular subjects – present tense)*

Komen jullie **uit** Duitsland of Oostenrijk?
Are you **from** Germany or Austria?

### 35 - over [prep, adv] *over; be left, extra*

Het lijkt erop dat de dieven **over** het hek zijn geklommen.
It seems like the thieves climbed **over** the fence.

### 36 - wat [pron] *what*

**Wat** willen de kinderen na het eten doen?
**What** do the children want to do after dinner?

### 37 - wordt [v] *to become; to get + adjective (2ⁿᵈ and 3ʳᵈ person singular -present tense; also used as the*

*auxiliary verb for perfect tenses)*

Klimaatverandering **wordt** ieder jaar erger.
Climate change **is getting** worse every year.

### 38 - heeft [v] *has, have (2<sup>nd</sup> and 3<sup>rd</sup> person - present tense)*

Zij **heeft** een vakantiehuisje in Spanje.
She **has** a holiday house in Spain.

### 39 - kan [n, v] *jug; can, to be able to (singular subjects - present tense)*

Mijn broer **kan** heel goed tekenen en voetballen.
My brother **can** draw and play football very well.

### 40 - ze [pron] *she; her; they; them*

Lopen **ze** iedere dag naar school of gaan **ze** met de fiets?
Do **they** walk to school every day or do **they** go by bike?

### 41 - nog [adv] *still; yet; more*

Werken jouw ouders **nog** steeds of zijn ze al met pensioen?
Are your parents **still** working or have they already retired?

### 42 - meer [n, adv] *lake; more*

Zou je niet graag wat **meer** tijd voor jezelf willen hebben?
Wouldn't you like to have some **more** time for yourself?

### 43 - tot [prep, adv] *to, until*

Op vrijdag werkt ons team maar **tot** 4 uur. Dat is heel fijn!
On Fridays our team only works **until** 4 o'clock. It's really nice!

### 44 - was [n, v] *laundry; to be (singular subjects in the*

*past tense)*

**Was** jij vorige week op vakantie in Los Angeles toen er een aardbeving **was**?
**Were** you on holiday in Los Angeles last week when there **was** an earthquake?

### 45 - hebben [v] *to have (infinitive and plural subjects - present tense)*

Jullie **hebben** twee weken om dit project af te maken.
You **have** two weeks to finish this project.

### 46 - hij [pron] *he*

Heeft **hij** net een koffie verkeerd besteld?
Did **he** just order a coffee with milk?

### 47 - zo [adv, conj] *this way; soon; so*

Mijn lerares heeft me geleerd om de sommen **zo** op te lossen.
My teacher has taught me to resolve the math exercises **this way**.

### 48 - kunnen [v] *can (infinitive and plural subjects - present tense)*

Misschien **kunnen** de buren ook wel meehelpen met het buurtfeest.
Maybe the neighbors **can** also help with the neighborhood party.

### 49 - al [adv, conj, pron] *already; even though; all*

Hebben jullie **al** ontbeten vanochtend?
Did you **already** have breakfast this morning?

### 50 - wel [n, adv, conj] *water source; certainly; sure; anyway; (also used for as the emphatic do/does, did)*

Mijn moeder denkt dat ik de koekjes **wel** heb gegeten, maar dat is

niet zo!
My mother thinks I **did** eat the cookies, but that's not the case!

### 51 - veel [adj, adv] *much, many; often, a lot*

In deze provincie zijn niet zo **veel** koeien.
In this province there aren't that **many** cows.

### 52 - uw [poss] *your (formal, singular and plural)*

Is dit **uw** koffer, meneer?
Is this **your** suitcase, sir?

### 53 - geen [art, adv] *not; no, none*

Hij zei dat hij **geen** idee had hoe laat het was.
He said he had **no** idea what time it was.

### 54 - mijn [poss, pron, n, v] *my; mine; mine; to mine (singular subject – present tense)*

Vorig jaar heb ik **mijn** studentenlening eindelijk afgelost.
Last year I finally paid off **my** student loan.

### 55 - jaar [n] *year*

Het eind van het **jaar** is in zicht!
The end of the **year** is in sight!

### 56 - wij [pron] *we*

**Wij** gaan over 2 weken verhuizen naar Groningen.
**We**'re moving to Groningen in 2 weeks.

### 57 - zich [pron] *to himself; herself; itself; themselves*

Ze vroeg **zich** af wat er met haar oude schoolvriendin was gebeurd.
She asked **herself** what had happened to her old classmate.

**58 - onze** [poss] *our*

We kunnen **onze** sleutels nergens vinden, help!
We can't find **our** keys anywhere, help!

**59 - goed** [n, adj, adv] *real estate; good; well; correct*

De klassieke Nederlandse film 'Turks Fruit' is heel **goed**!
The classic Dutch movie 'Turks Fruit' is really **good**!

**60 - ons** [pron, poss, n] *us; to ourselves; our; weight measurement for 100 grams*

Denk je dat de zanger **ons** zag zwaaien?
Do you think the singer saw **us** wave?

**61 - hun** [poss, pron] *their; to them*

We hebben **hun** jassen gevonden en meteen teruggegeven.
We found **their** coats and gave them straight back.

**62 - nu** [adv, conj] *(right) now; now that*

Ze zeiden dat ze **nu** geen tijd hadden om schoon te maken.
They said they didn't have time to clean **right now**.

**63 - na** [prep, adj, adv] *close; after*

**Na** het Sinterklaasfeest zit iedereen vol met snoep!
**After** the *Sinterklaas* party everyone is full of candy! *(traditional festivity celebrated in The Netherlands, based on Saint Nicholas, precursor of Santa Claus)*

**64 - andere** [n, adj] *(an)other; different*

Ik vind deze bloes niet mooi, kan je mij die **andere** aangeven?
I don't like this blouse; can you pass me that **other** one?

14

**65 - haar** [poss, pron, n] *her; her; hair*

Wanneer heb je **haar** voor het laatst gezien?
When was the last time you saw **her**?

**66 - waar** [n, adj, adv, conj] *ware; where; true; whereas*

**Waar** verkopen ze de beste friet met mayonaise in deze stad?
**Where** do they sell the best chips with mayonnaise in this city?

**67 - maken** [v] *to make, to fix (infinitive and plural subjects - present tense)*

Kan ik een afspraak **maken** met Meneer van Driel voor morgenochtend?
Can I **make** an appointment with Mr. van Driel for tomorrow morning?

**68 - weer** [n, adv] *weather; again*

Gaat je vriendin nou **weer** een nieuwe taal leren?
Is your (girl)friend going to learn a new language **again**?

**69 - alle** [pron] *all*

We hebben **alle** moeilijke vragen beantwoord.
We have answered **all** the difficult questions.

**70 - moet** [v] *must (singular subjects - present tense)*

De regering **moet** snel reageren op het migratieprobleem.
The government **must** react to the migration issue soon.

**71 - gaan** [v] *go; be possible (infinitive and plural subjects - present tense)*

De kinderen **gaan** van maandag tot en met vrijdag naar school.
The children **go** to school from Monday to Friday.

### 72 - dus [conj] *so; that's why*

Hun wekker ging niet af, **dus** ze kwamen te laat op hun werk!
Their alarm clock didn't go off, **so** they were late for work!

### 73 - nieuwe [adj] *new*

Volgende week gaan we in het **nieuwe** Indonesische restaurant eten.
Next week we're going to eat at the **new** Indonesian restaurant.

### 74 - kunt [v] *can (2$^{nd}$ and 3$^{rd}$ person - present tense)*

Jij **kunt** die liedjes zo mooi zingen!
You **can** sing those songs so beautifully!

### 75 - heb [v] *to have (1$^{st}$ and 2$^{nd}$ person - present tense)*

Ik **heb** geen energie om het huis schoon te maken vandaag.
I don't **have** any energy to clean the house today.

### 76 - hoe [adv] *how*

**Hoe** maak je de lekkerste stamppot?
**How** do you make the tastiest *stamppot? (Traditional Dutch dish)*

### 77 - werd [v] *to become; to get + adjective (singular subjects - past tense)*

Toen ik net begon met schaatsen, **werd** ik er heel snel moe van!
When I just started ice-skating, I **got** tired really quickly.

### 78 - mensen [n] *people*

Hoeveel **mensen** wonen er in jouw buurt?
How many **people** live in your neighborhood?

### 79 - gaat [v] *to go (2<sup>nd</sup> and 3<sup>rd</sup> person - present tense)*

Mijn neef **gaat** twee keer per week naar de sportschool.
My cousin **goes** to the gym twice a week.

### 80 - hier [adv] *here*

Kunt u **hier** op de stippellijn tekenen, alstublieft?
Can you sign **here** on the dotted line, please?

### 81 - zal [v] *shall, will (1<sup>st</sup> and 2<sup>nd</sup> person - future tense)*

Ik **zal** jouw zusje met haar wiskunde-huiswerk helpen.
I **will** help your sister with her math homework.

### 82 - onder [prep] *under*

**Onder** die grote appelboom is er een lekkere, frisse schaduw.
**Under** that big apple tree there's a nice, fresh shade.

### 83 - eerste [n, adj] *first*

Wie won de **eerste** plaats in de judowedstrijd?
Who won the **first** place in the judo competition?

### 84 - daar [adv] *(over) there*

De glazen staan **daar** in de keukenkast, naast de kopjes.
The glasses are over **there** in the kitchen cabinet, next to the cups.

### 85 - doen [v] *to do; to function (infinitive and plural subjects - present tense)*

Zullen we samen de afwas **doen**?
Shall we **do** the dishes together?

### 86 - alleen [adj, adv] *alone; only*

Het is helemaal niet erg om soms **alleen** te willen zijn.

It's not a bad thing to want to be **alone** sometimes.

### 87 - zij [prep, n] *she; they; side*

**Zij** speelt niet alleen heel mooi viool, maar heeft ook een geweldige stem!
**She** not only plays the violin beautifully, but also has an amazing voice!

### 88 - heel [adj, adv, v] *entire, whole; very; to heal (1ˢᵗ and 2ⁿᵈ person - present tense)*

De mensen op de universiteit waren **heel** aardig.
The people at the university were **very** friendly.

### 89 - zoals [conj] *(such) as; like*

Nederland produceert veel zuivelproducten, **zoals** melk, kaas, yoghurt en boter.
The Netherlands produce a lot of dairy products, **such as** milk, cheese, yogurt and butter.

### 90 - eigen [adj] **own**

Hebben hun kinderen ieder hun **eigen** slaapkamer?
Do their children each have their **own** bedroom?

### 91 - komen [v] *to come (infinitive and plural subjects - present tense)*

**Komen** jullie Australische oom en tante ook op jullie verjaardagsfeest?
Are your Australian uncle and aunt also **coming** to your birthday party?

### 92 - tijd [n] *time*

Mijn baas komt altijd op precies dezelfde **tijd** naar het werk.

My boss always comes to work at exactly the same **time**.

### 93 - zou [v] *shall; would; will (singular subjects - conditional tense)*

Jij **zou** dit dorpje aan de kust heel mooi vinden.
You **would** really like this village on the coast.

### 94 - zelf [pron, n] *(my, your, him, her)-self; self*

Mijn zus vindt het leuk om **zelf** kleren te ontwerpen.
My sister likes designing clothes **herself**.

### 95 - staat [n, v] *state; to stand; to be written (2nd and 3rd person - present tense)*

De kast **staat** tussen de trap en het bureau.
The closet is **standing** in between the stairs and the desk.

### 96 - twee [num] *two*

Was haar nichtje Marieke niet naar Brazilië verhuisd **twee** jaar geleden?
Didn't her cousin Marieke move to Brazil **two** years ago?

### 97 - ben [v] *to be (1st and 2nd person - present tense)*

Ik **ben** meestal heel zelfverzekerd, maar vanochtend was ik heel nerveus.
I **am** usually very confident, but this morning I was very nervous.

### 98 - wil [n, v] *will; to want (singular subjects - present tense)*

**Wil** jij ook mee naar de bioscoop morgenavond?
Do you also **want** to come along to the cinema tomorrow night?

19

**99 - mee** [adv] *along, together with*

Vroeger aten kinderen niet **mee** met de ouders.
In the past, children wouldn't eat **together** with their parents.

**100 - grote** [adj] *big*

Het jongetje schrok toen hij die hele **grote** hond zag.
The little boy got scared when he saw that really **big** dog.

**101 - toch** [adv] *anyway, after all; right?*

Dit is je nieuwe pen, **toch**?
This is your new pen, **right**?

**102 - had** [v] *to have (singular subjects - past tense)*

Jouw snackbar **had** de beste frietjes van deze stad.
Your fast-food restaurant **had** the best French fries in town.

**103 - zien** [v] *to see (infinitive and plural subjects - present tense)*

**Zien** zij hun ex-collega's nog weleens?
Do they ever **see** their ex-coworkers?

**104 - tegen** [prep, adv] *against*

De meeste mensen waren **tegen** het idee van de burgemeester.
The majority of people were **against** the mayor's idea.

**105 - per** [prep] *per, a; starting from*

De dokter zei tegen me dat ik drie keer **per** week moest sporten.
The doctor told me that I had to play sports three times **a** week.

**106 - via** [prep] *via, through*

Deze trein gaat naar Utrecht **via** Station Gouda.
This train goes to Utrecht **via** Gouda Station.

### 107 - komt [v] *to come (2<sup>nd</sup> and 3<sup>rd</sup> person - present tense)*

De secretaresse **komt** bijna altijd op tijd naar haar kantoor.
The secretary almost always **comes** to the office on time.

### 108 - dag [n, conj] *day; hello, bye*

We gaan nu naar het concert, **dag**!
We're now going to the concert, **bye**!

### 109 - omdat [conj] *because*

Mensen in Nederland rijden minder auto, **omdat** ze veel fietsen.
People in The Netherlands use their car less, **because** they cycle a lot.

### 110 - tussen [prep] *between*

Hij zei dat hij morgen **tussen** twee en vier uur 's middags langs zou komen.
He said he would drop by **between** two and four in the afternoon tomorrow.

### 111 - binnen [prep] *inside, within*

Het is erg koud vandaag, laten we **binnen** gaan zitten.
It's very cold today, let's go sit **inside**.

### 112 - tijdens [prep] *during*

Bel me alsjeblieft niet **tijdens** mijn yogales.
Please don't call me **during** my yoga class.

### 113 - moeten [v] *to have to, must (infinitive and plural subjects - present tense)*

Hoe lang **moeten** jullie nog werken voordat de vakantie begint?
How much longer do you **have to** work before the holidays start?

**114 - uur** [n] *hour; o'clock*

Iedere les duurt één **uur**.
Every class lasts one **hour**.

**115 - altijd** [adv] *always; at any time*

Naar het strand gaan is **altijd** heel ontspannend.
Going to the beach is **always** really relaxing.

**116 - mogelijk** [adj, adv] *possible; maybe*

Het is ook **mogelijk** om met een creditcard te betalen.
It's also **possible** to pay with a credit card.

**117 - verder** [adj, conj] *further; apart from*

We zijn er bijna, het is nog ietsje **verder**.
We're almost there, it's just a little bit **further**.

**118 - mij** [pron] *me*

Willen jullie **mij** nog vragen stellen?
Would you like to ask **me** any questions?

**119 - aantal** [n] *(unknown) amount, number*

Er was een groot **aantal** mensen op het Lowlands Festival dit jaar.
There was a large **amount** of people at Lowlands Festival this year.

**120 - kinderen** [n] *children*

De **kinderen** gaan van maandag tot en met vrijdag naar de crèche.
The **children** go to daycare from Monday to Friday.

**121 - iets** [pron, adv] *something; a little bit*

Ik wou dat we **iets** langer konden blijven.

I wish we could stay **a little bit** longer!

## 122 - eens [adj, adv] *agreed; once upon a time; at some point in the future*

De vriendinnen waren het nooit met elkaar **eens**.
The friends never **agreed** with each other.

## 123 - laten [v] *leave; let; let's (infinitive and plural subjects - present tense)*

**Laten** we morgen-ochtend beginnen met joggen!
**Let's** start jogging tomorrow morning!

## 124 - verschillende [adv] *different; several*

In de dierentuin zijn heel veel **verschillende** dieren.
At the zoo there are many **different** animals.

## 125 - af [adj, prep] *finished; away from; off of*

Wanneer denken jullie dat jullie nieuwe huis **af** zal zijn?
When do you think your new house will be **finished**?

## 126 - goede [adj] *good, well, correct*

Zijn dat wel de **goede** sleutels?
Are those the **correct** keys?

## 127 - een [num] *one; a*

De leerling stelt de leraar nog **een** laatste vraag.
The student asks the teacher **one** last question.

## 128 - samen [adv] *together*

De tweeling deed altijd alles **samen,** totdat ze allebei trouwden.
The twins always did everything **together** until they both got married.

### 129 - steeds [adv] *constantly, all the time*

De baby gooide haar eten **steeds** weer op de grond.
The baby **constantly** threw her food back on the floor.

### 130 - alles [n] *everything*

De mevrouw had **alles** geprobeerd, maar ze kon niet afvallen.
The lady tried **everything**, but she couldn't lose weight.

### 131 - gebruik [n, v] *use, to use (1$^{st}$ and 2$^{nd}$ person - present tense)*

Die oude windmolen is niet meer in **gebruik**.
That old windmill is no longer in **use**.

### 132 - want [n, conj] *mitten; because*

Mijn vriend wil niet naar New York, **want** hij haat vliegen.
My (boy)friend doesn't want to go to New York, **because** he hates flying.

### 133 - Nederland [n] *The Netherlands*

In **Nederland** zijn er heel veel koeien.
In **The Netherlands** there are lots of cows.

### 134 - me [pron] *me; to me*

Mijn moeder heeft **me** gisteren vanuit Polen gebeld.
My mother called **me** yesterday from Poland.

### 135 - hem [pron] *him; to him*

Kan je **hem** deze sleutels geven?
Can you give **him** these keys?

### 136 - leven [n, v] *life; to live; to be alive; (infinitive and*

*plural subjects -present tense)*

Heel veel millennials kunnen niet zonder smartphone **leven**.
A lot of millennials can't **live** without a smartphone.

### 137 - vaak [prep] *often*

Mijn zus eet **vaak** in hetzelfde restaurant op de hoek.
My sister **often** eats at the same restaurant on the corner.

### 138 - informatie [noun] *information*

Kunt u mij wat **informatie** over het Anne Frank Huis geven?
Could you give me some **information** about the Anne Frank House?

### 139 - waren [n, v] *wares; to be (plural subjects - past tense)*

We **waren** helaas niet op tijd voor de voetbalwedstrijd.
Unfortunately, we **weren't** on time for the soccer match.

### 140 - staan [v] *to stand; to be written (infinitive and plural subjects - present tense)*

Er **staan** vijftien mensen in de rij voor me!
There are fifteen people **standing** in line before me!

### 141 - even [prep, adv] *even (even number, flat); quickly, easily*

Jaap gaat **even** op de fiets naar de markt.
Jaap is going to the market by bike **quickly**.

### 142 - plaats [n, v] *place; space, room; square; to place (1st and 2nd person - present tense)*

Het model had niet genoeg **plaats** in haar koffer.

The model didn't have enough **room** in her suitcase.

### 143 - elkaar [pron] *each other*

Het pasgetrouwde echtpaar is dol op **elkaar**.
The newlyweds love **each other** like crazy.

### 144 - geven [v] *to give (infinitive and plural subjects - present tense)*

Wat zullen we onze kleinkinderen dit jaar voor Kerst **geven**?
What shall we **give** our grandchildren for Christmas this year?

### 145 - zonder [prep] *without*

Wilt u uw frietjes met of **zonder** mayonaise?
Would you like your fries with or **without** mayonnaise?

### 146 - wanneer [adv, conj] *when, whenever*

**Wanneer** is Suriname onafhankelijk geworden?
**When** did Suriname become independent?

### 147 - zeer [n, adj, adv] *pain; very; painful*

Veel Nederlanders spreken **zeer** goed Engels.
Many Dutch people speak **very** good English.

### 148 - werken [n, v] *works; to function; to work (infinitive and plural subjects - present tense)*

De meeste mensen **werken** van maandag tot en met vrijdag.
Most people **work** from Monday to Friday.

### 149 - gemaakt [v] *fixed; made (past participle)*

Mijn zoontje heeft een hele mooie tekening voor mij **gemaakt**!
My little son has **made** a beautiful drawing for me!

**150 - werk** [n, v] *work; to work (1ˢᵗ and 2ⁿᵈ person - present tense)*

Waar **werk** jij tegenwoordig?
Where do you **work** nowadays?

**151 - echt** [n, adj, adv] *marriage; real; really, truly*

De documentaire was **echt** prachtig.
The documentary was **really** beautiful.

**152 - snel** [adj, adv] *quick; quickly*

De regenbui was gelukkig **snel** afgelopen.
Thankfully, the rain was over **quickly**.

**153 - nodig** [adj] *necessary*

Het is niet **nodig** om je paspoort in de trein bij je te hebben.
It's not **necessary** to have your passport on you on the train.

**154 - vanaf** [prep] *from*

De Dam is ongeveer tien minuten lopen **vanaf** hier.
Dam square is about ten minutes walking **from** here.

**155 - vinden** [v] *to find; to think (as in opinion) (infinitive and plural subjects - present tense)*

Buitenlandse toeristen **vinden** Nederlandse drop meestal niet lekker.
Foreign tourists usually don't **think** Dutch licorice is very tasty.

**156 - toe** [adj, adv, conj] *to, towards; closed; come on*

Hij ging naar het huis van zijn vriendin **toe** na zijn werk.
He went **to** his girlfriend's house after work.

**157 - website** [n] *website*

Het bedrijf heeft net een nieuwe **website** laten maken.

The company just had a new **website** made.

**158 - natuurlijk** [adj, adv] *natural; of course*

**Natuurlijk** mogen jullie hier blijven slapen vanavond!

**Of course** you can stay over here tonight!

**159 - bijvoorbeeld** [adv] *for example*

Deze bakkerij verkoopt gebak, **bijvoorbeeld** appelflappen en kersenvlaai.

This bakery sells pastries, **for example**, apple turnovers and cherry pie.

**160 - willen** [v] *to want (infinitive and plural subjects - present tense)*

Hoe laat **willen** de mensen morgen vertrekken?

What time do the people **want** to leave tomorrow?

**161 - keer** [n, v] *time (as in repetition, or multiplication); to turn around (1st and 2nd person -present tense)*

Mijn oma heeft Alzheimer en vergeet iedere **keer** dat ik haar zie, mijn naam.

My grandma has Alzheimer's and forgets my name every **time** I see her.

**162 - erg** [n, adj, adv] *notice; awful; very*

Het centrum van Amsterdam is **erg** schilderachtig.

The Amsterdam city center is **very** picturesque.

**163 - toen** [conj, adv] *when; (back) then*

De tieners gingen naar huis **toen** het concert was afgelopen.

28

The teenagers went home **when** the concert had finished.

**164 - krijgen** [v] *to receive, to get; to obtain (infinitive and plural subjects - present tense)*

Bekende zangers **krijgen** meestal heel veel e-mails van fans.
Famous singers usually **get** a lot of emails from fans.

**165 - laat** [adv, v] *late; to let (singular subjects - present tense)*

Zorg dat je niet te **laat** op school komt morgen!
Make sure not to be **late** for school tomorrow!

**166 - bent** [v] *are (2^{nd} and 3^{rd} person - present tense)*

U **bent** de beste geschiedenisleraar die ik ooit gehad heb!
You **are** the best history teacher I've ever had!

**167 - terug** [prep, adv] *ago; again; return, back; backwards*

Geef alsjeblieft het jongetje zijn autootje **terug**.
Please give the boy **back** his toy car.

**168 - vooral** [adv] *especially, primarily*

Het regent veel in Nederland, **vooral** in de winter.
It rains a lot in The Netherlands, **especially** in winter.

**169 - weg** [n, prep] *road, way; away, gone*

Tim is nu al drie maanden **weg** uit de buurt.
Tim has been **gone** from the neighborhood for three months now.

**170 - jaren** [n] *years*

In Gouda wordt kaas al vele **jaren** op dezelfde manier gemaakt.
In Gouda, cheese is being made in the same way for many **years**.

**171 - maakt** [v] *make; fix (2<sup>nd</sup> and 3<sup>rd</sup> person - present tense)*

Kom wanneer je wil, het **maakt** niet veel uit.
Come whenever you want, it doesn't **make** much of a difference.

**172 - laatste** [n, adj] *last; latest*

Radio 538 speelt altijd de **laatste** pop-hits.
Radio 538 always plays the **latest** pop hits.

**173 - zullen** [v] *shall; will (probably) (infinitive and plural subjects - future tense)*

Na het wereldkampioenschap **zullen** de spelers wel vakantie willen.
After the World Cup, the players **will probably** want to go on holiday.

**174 - welke** [pron] *which*

**Welke** broek vond hij mooier, de bruine of de zwarte?
**Which** pants did he find more beautiful, the brown or the black ones?

**175 - men** [pron, v] *one (as in an impersonal group of people); they*

Wat zal **men** wel niet denken van je nieuwe kapsel?
What will **people** think of your new haircut?

**176 - manier** [n] *way (as in manner of doing something)*

De actrice had een hele excentrieke **manier** van kleden.
The actress had a very eccentric **way** of dressing.

**177 - groot** [adj, adv] *big; great; important; adult*

Deze koffer is niet **groot** genoeg voor al mijn kleren.

This suitcase isn't **big** enough for all of my clothes.

### 178 - net [n, adj, adv] *net; network; tidy; just; just like*

Jullie zijn **net** op tijd, want de parade begint om 2 uur.
You have arrived **just** in time, because the parade starts at 2 o'clock.

### 179 - foto [n] *photography, print*

Hier hangt een prachtige **foto** van het IJsselmeer.
Here's a beautiful **photo** of Lake IJssel.

### 180 - minder [adj, v] *less; to decrease (1$^{st}$ and 2$^{nd}$ person - present tense)*

**Minder** vlees eten is meestal goed voor de gezondheid.
Eating **less** meat is usually good for one's health.

### 181 - drie [num] *three*

De buren hebben **drie** kinderen: Marieke, Janneke en Paul.
The neighbors have **three** children: Marieke, Janneke, and Paul.

### 182 - wie [pron] *who*

**Wie** heeft jou om drie uur 's nachts gebeld gisteren?
**Who** called you at three in the morning yesterday?

### 183 - hebt [v] *to have (2$^{nd}$ person - present tense)*

Jij **hebt** een hele mooie stem!
You **have** a very beautiful voice!

### 184 - zeker [adj] *sure; surely; certain*

Weet ze **zeker** dat ze met die man wil trouwen?
Is she **sure** she wants to marry that man?

31

### 185 - hele [adj, adv] *entire, whole; very*

De kat van onze buren was de **hele** nacht aan het miauwen.
Our neighbor's cat was meowing the **entire** night.

### 186 - graag [adv] *gladly, willingly*

Onze receptioniste helpt u **graag** indien u een probleem heeft.
Our receptionist will **gladly** assist you in case you have a problem.

### 187 - vragen [n, v] *questions; to ask (infinitive and plural subjects - present tense)*

De leerlingen **vragen** hun leraar over de inhoud van het examen.
The students **ask** their teacher about the contents of the exam.

### 188 - iedereen [pron] *everyone, everybody*

Heeft **iedereen** al een stukje cake op?
Has **everyone** had a piece of cake?

### 189 - weet [v] *to know (singular subjects - present tense)*

**Weet** u hoeveel een taxi naar het station kost?
Do you **know** how much a taxi to the station costs?

### 190 - nemen [v] *to take (infinitive and plural subjects - present tense)*

Iedere dag **nemen** duizenden mensen de trein naar hun werk.
Every day, thousands of people **take** the train to work.

### 191 - beter [adj] *better, healthy again*

Welke van deze twee hotels is **beter**?
Which of these two hotels is **better**?

**192 - elke** [pron] *every, each*

Gaan ze nog steeds **elke** week naar dezelfde bar?
Are they still going to the same bar **every** week?

**193 - zelfs** [adv] *even*

In Nederland fietsen mensen **zelfs** als het regent.
In The Netherlands, people **even** cycle when it's raining.

**194 - weten** [v] *to know; to realize (infinitive and plural subjects - present tense)*

We **weten** niets af van fotografie!
We don't **know** anything about photography!

**195 - geeft** [v] *to give ($2^{nd}$ and $3^{rd}$ person - present tense)*

De overheid **geeft** een woningsubsidie aan mensen zonder inkomen.
The government **gives** subsidized housing to people without an income.

**196 - week** [n, adj, v] *week; soft; to soak ($1^{st}$ and $2^{nd}$ person - present tense)*

Volgende **week** is mijn mans verjaardag!
Next **week** is my husband's birthday!

**197 - volgende** [adj] *next; following*

De **volgende** patiënt mag nu binnen-komen!
The **next** patient can come in now!

**198 - houden** [v] *to hold; to keep; to continue (infinitive and plural subjects - present tense)*

De kinderen mochten de grote ballonnen **houden.**

33

The children could **keep** the large balloons.

### 199 - enkele [adj, adv] *single; some, a few*

We hebben **enkele** opmerkingen over het onderhoud van het huis.
We have **a few** comments about the maintenance of the house.

### 200 - huis [n] *house*

Het **huis** van de heks was van snoep gemaakt.
The witch's **house** was made of candy.

### 201 - echter [adj, conj] *more real; however, nevertheless*

Ik ben dol op skiën; je kan het **echter** alleen in de winter doen.
I love skiing; **however,** you can only do it in winter.

### 202 - deel [n, v] *part; to divide, to share (1<sup>st</sup> and 2<sup>nd</sup> person - present tense)*

Ik **deel** altijd mijn favoriete bonbons met mijn collega's.
I always **share** my favorite chocolates with my coworkers.

### 203 - ten [prep] *at the, of the (roughly translates to "of the" or "at the" but sounds old-fashioned and is mainly used in set expressions)*

**Ten** huize van de familie Van Veen werd altijd veel gezongen.
**At the** home of the van Veen's there was always a lot of singing.

### 204 - kun [v] *can (only for 2<sup>nd</sup> person in present tense questions)*

**Kun** jij mij op je brommer naar de stad brengen?
**Can** you take me into town on your motorbike?

**205 - volgens** [prep] *according to*

Volgens het weerbericht gaat het morgen regenen.
According to the weather forecast, it'll rain tomorrow.

**206 - mag** [v] *may; to be allowed to; to like someone (singular subjects - present tense)*

Mag ik deze doos in de recycling-bak doen?
Am I allowed to put this box in the recycling bin?

**207 – mooie** [adj] *pretty, beautiful*

Er zijn vijf hele mooie nieuwe schilderijen in het stadsmuseum.
There are five very pretty new paintings at the city museum.

**208 - naast** [adj, prep] *close; next to*

De schoenenwinkel zit naast de kledingwinkel.
The shoe store is next to the clothes store.

**209 - vanuit** [prep] *from*

Het speelgoed wordt naar heel Europa geëxporteerd vanuit de fabriek in Denemarken.
The toys are exported to all of Europe from the factory in Denmark.

**210 - zodat** [conj] *so that; in order to*

Topatleten eten koolhydraten zodat ze genoeg energie hebben.
Top athletes eat a lot of carbohydrates so that they have enough energy.

**211 - kleine** [n, adj] *small one; small, little*

Mijn ouders houden alleen van kleine hondjes.
My parents only like small dogs.

**212 - anders** [adv, conj] *other; different; in other circumstances; if not*

Vandaag wil ik geen aardappelen met biefstuk, ik wil iets **anders!**
Today I don't want potatoes with steak, I want something **different!**

**213 - vraag** [n, v] *question; to demand; to ask (1ˢᵗ and 2ⁿᵈ person - present tense)*

Ik weet het antwoord op die **vraag** helaas niet.
Unfortunately, I don't know the answer to that **question.**

**214 - wilt** [v] *to want (3ʳᵈ person - present tense)*

**Wilt** u met creditcard of contant betalen?
Do you **want** to pay by credit card or cash?

**215 - werden** [v] *to become; get + adjective (plural subjects - past tense; also used as the auxiliary verb for perfect tenses)*

**Werden** houten klompen vroeger echt op het veld gebruikt?
**Were** wooden clogs really used in the fields in the past?

**216 - daarom** [adv] *because, therefore, that's why, hence*

Ik ga naar België verhuizen, **daarom** leer ik Nederlands.
I'm moving to Belgium, **that's why** I'm learning Dutch.

**217 - zit** [v] *to sit; to be in a certain place or situation (singular subjects - present tense, also used to form the present continuous tense)*

**Zit** mijn portemonnee in mijn rugzak?
**Is** my wallet in my backpack?

**218 - water** [n] *water, to water (1ˢᵗ and 2ⁿᵈ person –*

*present tense)*

Veel mensen drinken niet genoeg **water** en te veel koffie.
Many people don't drink enough **water** and too much coffee.

### 219 - extra [adj] *extra*

Het voetbalteam had **extra** hard getraind voor de belangrijke wedstrijd.
The soccer team trained **extra** hard for the important match.

### 220 - beste [n, adj, adv] *best; dear*

Marjolein en Joris zijn **beste** vrienden sinds de basisschool!
Marjolein and Joris have been **best** friends since elementary school!

### 221 - vindt [v] *to find; to think (as in opinion) (2<sup>nd</sup> and 3<sup>rd</sup> person - present tense)*

Mijn moeder **vindt** altijd hele leuke dingen in tweedehands-winkels.
My mother always **finds** really cute things in second-hand stores.

### 222 - tweede [n, adj] *second (ordinal number)*

Het Nederlandse parlement bestaat uit de Eerste Kamer en de **Tweede** Kamer.
The Dutch Parliament consists of the First Chamber and the **Second** Chamber.

### 223 - krijgt [v] *to receive, to get; to obtain (2<sup>nd</sup> and 3<sup>rd</sup> person - present tense)*

Mijn zusje **krijgt** leuke cadeautjes op 5 december vanwege Sinterklaas.
My sister **gets** nice presents on the 5th of December because of *Sinterklaas*.

**224 - zowel** [adv] *as well as; both*

Drop is **zowel** populair in Nederland als in België.
Licorice is popular in The Netherlands **as well as** in Belgium.

**225 - gebruikt** [v] *to use (2$^{nd}$ and 3$^{rd}$ person - present tense; past participle)*

De Nederlandse komiek Arjen Lubach **gebruikt** veel slimme woordgrapjes.
The Dutch comedian, Arjen Lubach, **uses** a lot of clever puns.

**226 - onderzoek** [n, v] *research; to research; to examine (1$^{st}$ and 2$^{nd}$ person - present tense)*

Er moet nog meer **onderzoek** komen naar de oorzaken van fibromyalgie.
More **research** has to be done into the causes of fibromyalgia.

**227 - gewoon** [adj, adv] *normal; simply; as usual*

Dit spreekwoord beschrijft Nederlanders goed: Doe maar **gewoon**, dan doe je al gek genoeg.
This proverb describes Dutch people well: Just act **normal**, you'll be acting crazy enough.

**228 - kwam** [v] *to come (singular subjects - past tense)*

Onze opa **kwam** ook weleens op bezoek bij ons in Engeland.
Our granddad also **came** to visit us in England at times.

**229 - wereld** [n] *world*

Is jouw droom ook om de hele **wereld** rond te reizen?
Is your dream also to travel around the whole **world**?

**230 - allemaal** [pron] *everything, all*

Deze producten worden **allemaal** in China geproduceerd.

These products are **all** produced in China.

### 231 - jullie [pron, poss] *you (p); your (p)*

Hebben **jullie** genoeg gegeten of willen **jullie** nog wat meer?
Have **you** eaten enough, or would **you** like some more?

### 232 - moment [n] *moment*

Eén **moment** alstublieft, ik ben zo bij u.
One **moment** please, I'll be right with you.

### 233 - helemaal [adv] *entirely, completely, totally*

Oh nee, ik ben mijn huissleutels **helemaal** vergeten!
Oh no, I've **completely** forgotten my house keys!

### 234 - eerst [adv] *first, before; at first*

Op zijn werk bekijkt hij **eerst** zijn e-mail.
At work, he **first** checks his email.

### 235 - kon [v] *can, to be able to (singular subjects - past tense)*

De dokter **kon** de patiënt niet goed verstaan.
The physician **couldn't** understand the patient very well.

### 236 - blijven [v] *to stay (infinitive and plural subjects - present tense)*

Hoe lang zullen de diplomaten in het land **blijven**?
How long will the diplomats **stay** in the country?

### 237 - zie [v] *to see (1ˢᵗ and 2ⁿᵈ person - present tense)*

**Zie** je die bloemen daar? Het zijn allemaal tulpen!
Do you **see** those flowers over there? They're all tulips!

### 238 - dagen [n, v] *days; to dawn; to summon in court (infinitive and plural subjects - present tense)*

Hoeveel **dagen** per week werken de verpleegkundigen?

How many **days** a week do the nurses work?

### 239 - bedrijf [n] *business, company*

Shell is al jarenlang het grootste Nederlandse **bedrijf**.

Shell has been the largest Dutch **company** for years.

### 240 - lang [adj] *long, tall*

De meeste Nederlandse mannen zijn heel **lang**.

The majority of Dutch men are very **tall**.

### 241 - ligt [v] *to lie; to be situated (2$^{nd}$ and 3$^{rd}$ person - present tense)*

Den Haag **ligt** vijfenvijftig kilometer verwijderd van Utrecht.

The Hague **is situated** fifty-five kilometers from Utrecht.

### 242 - waarin [adv] *in which*

Dit is het huis **waarin** Anne Frank en haar familie hebben gewoond.

This is the house **in which** Anne Frank and her family lived.

### 243 - doet [v] *to do; to function (2$^{nd}$ and 3$^{rd}$ person - present tense)*

**Doet** die afstandsbediening het nog wel?

Is that remote control still **functioning**?

### 244 - jij [pron] *you (s)*

Heb **jij** één of twee voornamen?

Do **you** have one or two first names?

**245 - vele** [adj] *much, many*

Nog **vele** jaren geluk-gewenst!
We wish you **many** more happy years!

**246 - vind** [v] *to find; to think (as in opinion) (1<sup>st</sup> and 2<sup>nd</sup> person - present tense)*

**Vind** jij weleens geld op straat?
Do you ever **find** money on the street?

**247 - gemeente** [n] *municipality; congregation; community*

In mijn **gemeente** wordt heel veel aandacht besteed aan het openbaar groen.
In my **municipality**, a lot of emphasis is put on public green spaces.

**248 - daarnaast** [adv] *besides, furthermore; next to it*

Zie je die ijssalon? **Daarnaast** zit de computerwinkel.
Do you see that ice cream parlor? **Next to it** is the computer store.

**249 - belangrijk** [adj] *important; considerable amount of*

Dijken zijn in Nederland heel erg **belangrijk**!
Dikes are very **important** in The Netherlands!

**250 - online** [adj, adv] *online*

Er is heel veel informatie **online** tegenwoordig.
There's a lot of information **online** nowadays.

**251 - nooit** [adv] *never*

Ben je echt nog **nooit** in de Efteling geweest?
Have you really **never** been to the *Efteling*? (*Dutch amusement park*)

41

**252 - waarbij** [adv] *whereby; with which; by which*

Mijn favoriete filmgenre is psychologische thrillers **waarbij** je veel moet denken.

My favorite film genre is psychological thrillers **with which** you have to think a lot.

**253 - euro** [n] *euro*

Vóór de **euro** was de gulden de munteenheid in Nederland.

Before the **euro**, the currency in The Netherlands was the guilder.

**254 - soms** [adv] *sometimes; perhaps*

**Soms** zie je konijnen en eekhoorns in dit park.

You **sometimes** see rabbits and squirrels in this park.

**255 - ter** [prep] *at the, of the (roughly translates to "of the" or "at the" but sounds old-fashioned and is mainly used in set expressions)*

Kleine wonden in het bouwproject worden **ter** plekke behandeld.

Small wounds at the building site are treated **on** site.

**256 - mooi** [adj] *pretty, beautiful; pleasant (for the weather)*

Wat is het **mooi** weer vandaag!

How **pleasant** the weather is today!

**257 - ging** [v] *to go; to be possible (singular subjects - past tense)*

De vrouw **ging** met haar man naar de sauna.

The woman **went** to the sauna with her husband.

**258 - diverse** [adj] *diverse; several; different*

Mijn halfzusje houdt van hele **diverse** muziekstijlen.

My half-sister likes very **different** styles of music.

### 259 - groep [n] *group; grade (year at school)*

Janine is lerares en geeft les in **groep** 6 van de basisschool.
Janine is a teacher and teaches 4th **grade** in elementary school.

### 260 - contact [n] *contact*

Mocht uw product niet werken, gelieve spoedig met ons **contact**
op te nemen.
In case your product doesn't work, please **contact** us swiftly.

### 261 - gebied [n, v] *area, region; to dictate (1st and 2nd person - present tense)*

De Biesbosch is een heel mooi **gebied** met veel natuur.
De Biesbosch is a very pretty **area** with lots of nature.

### 262 - the [art] *the (this is basically "the" in English, appearing here because English is used a lot by Dutch speakers in music, film etc)*

"Let **the** beat control your body" was één van de hits van pop-duo
2 Unlimited.
"Let **the** beat control your body" was one of the hits by pop-duo 2
Unlimited.

### 263 - lees [v] *to read (1st and 2nd person - present tense)*

**Lees** jij veel boeken?
Do you **read** many books?

### 264 - naam [n] *name, reputation*

Welke **naam** vind jij mooier, Amelie of Sophie?
Which **name** do you think is prettier, Amelie or Sophie?

**265 - achter** [prep] *behind*

We stonden **achter** 20 andere mensen in de rij!
We were standing **behind** 20 other people in the line!

**266 - leuk** [adj] *nice; fun; pleasant; funny*

Het personeelsfeestje van gisteravond was heel **leuk**.
Last night's staff party was a lot of **fun**.

**267 - geld** [n] *money*

"Tijd is **geld**" is het motto van de moderne tijd.
"Time is **money**" is the motto of the modern era.

**268 - ga** [v] *to go; to be possible (1ˢᵗ and 2ⁿᵈ person - present tense)*

Ik **ga** over twee maanden naar Madrid om Spaans te studeren.
I'm **going** to Madrid in two months to study Spanish.

**269 - direct** [adj, adv] *direct; straight(away)*

Kinderen, na school moeten jullie **direct** naar huis komen!
Kids, after school you have to come **straight** home!

**270 - rond** [prep, adj] *around; round*

De president zal morgen **rond** negen uur landen.
The president will land at **around** nine tomorrow.

**271 - niets** [pron] *nothing*

Er zat **niets** meer in de koektrommel, jammer!
There was **nothing** left in the cookie jar, too bad!

**272 - gebruiken** [n, v] *uses; to use (infinitive and plural*

Glazen flessen kan je altijd weer opnieuw **gebruiken**.
You can always **use** glass bottles again.

### 273 - open [adj, v] *open; to open (1ˢᵗ and 2ⁿᵈ person - present tense)*

De deuren van ons huis staan altijd **open** voor jou.
The doors of our house are always **open** for you.

### 274 - kennis [n] *acquaintance; knowledge*

De astronoom heeft veel **kennis** van het heelal.
The astronomer has a lot of **knowledge** about space.

### 275 - producten [n] *products*

In warenhuizen worden veel verschillende soorten **producten** verkocht.
Department stores sell many different types of **products**.

### 276 - organisatie [n] *organization*

Er zijn veel **organisaties** die dakloze mensen helpen.
There are many **organizations** that help the homeless.

### 277 - zorg [n, v] *care; the healthcare system; to take care of, to look after (1ˢᵗ and 2ⁿᵈ person - present tense)*

**Zorg** jij voor de frisdrank voor het feestje op vrijdag?
Will you **take care of** the soda for the party on Friday?

### 278 - geval [n] *case*

Voor het **geval** dat je denkt dat je te laat zal komen, hier is ons mobiele nummer.
In **case** you think you're going to be late, here is our cell phone number.

**279 - zitten** [v] *to sit, to be in a certain place or situation (infinitive and plural subjects - present tense; auxiliary verb to form the present continuous tense)*

De vogeltjes **zitten** zich te wassen.
The little birds **are washing** themselves.

**280 - kosten** [n, v] *costs; to cost (infinitive and plural subjects - present tense)*

Hoeveel **kosten** de vliegtickets naar Rome?
How much do the flight tickets to Rome **cost?**

**281 - misschien** [adv] *maybe; perhaps*

We verhuizen volgend jaar **misschien** naar Zweden.
**Perhaps** we'll move to Sweden next year.

**282 - kijken** [v] *to look; to watch (infinitive and plural subjects - present tense)*

Veel kinderen **kijken** tegenwoordig te veel TV.
Many children **watch** too much TV nowadays.

**283 - den** [n, art] *pine tree; of the (roughly translates to "of the" or "at the" but sounds old-fashioned and is mainly used in set expressions)*

Afvallen is moeilijk, maar als je doorzet, lukt het op **den** duur.
Losing weight is hard, but if you persist, in **the** end, you'll succeed.

**284 - der** [art] *the; of the (roughly translates to "of the" or "at the" but sounds old-fashioned and is mainly used in set expressions, slightly archaic)*

Veel Nederlandse achternamen beginnen met "van **der**".
Many Dutch last names start with "van der" (meaning: "**of the**").

**285 - m** [n, pron] *the letter m; 'm is also a very common contraction of "hem" which means "it" or "him"*

Hebben jullie 'm een kadootje gegeven voor zijn verjaardag?
Did you give **him** a present for his birthday?

**286 - boek** [n, v] *book; to book (1st and 2nd person - present tense)*

Dit **boek** heb ik bij de bibliotheek geleend.
I borrowed this **book** at the library.

**287 - lekker** [adj, adv] *tasty, delicious; deliciously; pleasant*

Traditionele Limburgse vlaaien zijn heel **lekker**!
Traditional pies from Limburg are very **tasty**!

**288 - blijft** [v] *to stay; to remain (2nd and 3rd person - present tense)*

Tot hoe laat **blijft** de verse groente en fruit markt open?
Until what time does the fresh fruit and vegetable market **stay** open?

**289 - spelen** [n, v] *games; to play (an instrument) (infinitive and plural subjects - present tense)*

Natuurlijk is met auto's **spelen** niet alleen voor jongens!
Of course, **playing** with cars isn't just for boys!

**290 - Nederlandse** [adj] *Dutch, used to refer to the Dutch language, nationality, and its citizens*

**Nederlandse** tulpen zijn over de hele wereld bekend.
**Dutch** tulips are famous all around the world.

**291 - oude** [n, adj, adv] *old one; old*

Hebben zij misschien **oude** kranten over?
Do they perhaps have some spare **old** newspapers?

**292 - bijna** [adv] *almost*

De actrice werd zo laat wakker dat ze **bijna** haar vlucht had gemist.
The actress woke up so late that she **almost** missed her flight.

**293 - waardoor** [adv] *because of which/that; whereby; through which*

Ik had te veel chilli bij de pastasaus gedaan **waardoor** het niet te eten was!
I had put too much chili in the pasta sauce and **because of that** it was inedible!

**294 - paar** [n, adj, v] *a couple; two; a set; to mate with someone (1ˢᵗ and 2ⁿᵈ person - present tense)*

Het is fijn om een **paar** dagen vrij te hebben.
It's nice to have **a couple** of days off.

**295 - auto** [n] *car*

Een elektrische **auto** is beter voor het milieu dan een normale auto.
An electric **car** is better for the environment than a normal car.

**296 - sinds** [prep, conj] *since*

België is **sinds** 1830 een onafhankelijk land.
Belgium has been an independent country **since** 1830.

**297 - vandaag** [adv] *today*

De leerlingen hebben **vandaag** vrij: het is Koningsdag.
The students have the day off school **today**: it's King's Day.

### 298 - ander [n, adj] *(an)other; different*

Mag ik een **ander** boek van je lenen?
Can I borrow a **different** book from you?

### 299 - later [adj, adv] *later*

Morgen gaan de schoonmakers wat **later** naar hun werk.
Tomorrow the cleaners will go to work a bit **later**.

### 300 - hadden [v] *to have (plural subjects - past tense)*

Tien jaar geleden **hadden** mensen simpelere mobiele telefoons.
Ten years ago, people **had** simpler cell phones.

### 301 - basis [n] *basis; foundation; base*

Veel mensen werken nu op zelfstandige **basis**.
Many people now work on a freelance **basis**.

### 302 - biedt [v] *to offer; to bid; to provide (2ⁿᵈ and 3ʳᵈ person - present tense)*

De schoenenwinkel **biedt** klanten op het moment 30% korting!
The shoe store is **offering** customers a 30% discount at the moment!

### 303 - duidelijk [adj] *clear*

Dit handschrift is niet **duidelijk**: het is onleesbaar.
This handwriting isn't **clear**: it's illegible.

### 304 - werkt [v] *to function; to work (2ⁿᵈ and 3ʳᵈ person - present tense)*

**Werkt** deze telefoonoplader nog?
Is this phone charger still **working**?

**305 - buiten** [prep, adv] *outside; except*

Het is voor kinderen gezond om veel **buiten** te spelen.
It's healthy for children to play **outside** a lot.

**306 - bestaat** [v] *to exist (2<sup>nd</sup> and 3<sup>rd</sup> person - present tense)*

Onze volleybalvereniging **bestaat** nu al 50 jaar.
Our volleyball club has now already **existed** for 50 years.

**307 - brengen** [v] *to bring (infinitive and plural subjects - present tense)*

Hoeveel koffers **brengen** jullie meestal op vakantie mee?
How many suitcases do you usually **bring** on holidays?

**308 - nieuw** [adj, adv] *new; fresh*

Heb je die jas **nieuw** of tweedehands gekocht?
Did you buy that coat **new** or secondhand?

**309 - meest** [n, adv] *(the) most; usually*

Wie eet er het **meest**, jij of je broer?
Who eats the **most**, you or your brother?

**310 - programma** [n] *(computer) program; television show; theatre/concert program; planning*

Mijn favoriete **programma** is op het moment TreurTeeVee.
My favorite **television show** at the moment is TreurTeeVee.

**311 - man** [n] *male; man; husband*

Sara ontmoette haar **man** tijdens een vakantie in Griekenland.
Sara met her **husband** during a holiday in Greece.

**312 - prijs** [n, v] *price; prize; to put a price on (1<sup>st</sup> and 2<sup>nd</sup>*

*person - present tense)*

Tachtig euro voor een fiets is een hele goede **prijs**!
Eighty euros for a bicycle is a very good **price**!

### 313 - eigenlijk [adj, adv] *actual; actually*

**Eigenlijk** hadden ze geen zin om schoon te maken.
They **actually** didn't feel like cleaning.

### 314 - gratis [adj, adv] *free (of charge)*

Mensen zijn dol op **gratis** dingen!
People are crazy about **free** stuff!

### 315 - iemand [pron] *someone*

Volgens mij is er **iemand** aan de deur.
I think there's **someone** at the door.

### 316 - school [n, v] *school; school of fish; to school (1ˢᵗ person - present tense)*

In Nederland moeten kinderen van vijf tot zestien jaar naar **school**.
In The Netherlands children aged five to sixteen have to attend **school**.

### 317 - waarom [adv] *why; the reason why*

**Waarom** zijn bananen niet recht?
**Why** aren't bananas straight?

### 318 - daarna [adv] *afterwards, after that, subsequently*

Eerst je huiswerk afmaken, **daarna** mag je pas TV kijken.
Finish your homework first, **after that** you can watch TV.

### 319 - kind [n] *child; son or daughter*

Dat arme **kind** speelde iedere dag urenlang computerspelletjes.

The poor **child** played video games for hours on end every day.

### 320 - zorgen [n, v] *worries; to take care of (infinitive and plural subjects - present tense)*

Wie **zorgen** er voor hun honden als ze op vakantie gaan?

Who **takes care of** their dogs when they go on holiday?

### 321 - hand [n] *hand*

Soms lopen de oudejaarsfeestjes een beetje uit de **hand**!

Sometimes New Year's Eve celebrations get a little out of **hand**!

### 322 - kwaliteit [n] *quality*

Veel producten uit China zijn van lage **kwaliteit**.

Many products from China are of low **quality**.

### 323 - zeggen [v] *to say; to mean (infinitive and plural subjects - present tense)*

Veel Nederlanders **zeggen** precies wat ze denken.

Many Dutch people **say** exactly what they are thinking.

### 324 - jouw [poss] *your*

Zijn dit **jouw** sleutels?

Are these **your** keys?

### 325 - bedrijven [n] *companies*

Veel internationale **bedrijven** hebben hun hoofdkantoor in Nederland.

Many international **companies** have their headquarters in The Netherlands.

### 326 - bieden [v] *to offer; to bid; to provide (infinitive and plural subjects - present tense)*

Niet alle restaurants **bieden** goedkopere dagmenu's aan.
Not all restaurants **offer** cheaper set menus.

### 327 - stad [n] *city*

Veel jongeren uit kleine dorpen verhuizen naar een grote **stad** om te studeren.
Many young people from small villages move to a big **city** to study.

### 328 - terwijl [conj] *while; even though*

Je mobiele telefoon gebruiken **terwijl** je autorijdt is heel gevaarlijk!
Using your cell phone **while** you drive is very dangerous!

### 329 - gedaan [v] *done (past participle)*

Wij hebben de meerderheid van het werk **gedaan**.
We've **done** the majority of the work.

### 330 - ervaring [n] *experience*

Voor vertalers is **ervaring** vaak belangrijker dan een diploma.
For translators, **experience** is often more important than a diploma.

### 331 - geweest [v] *been (past participle)*

Mijn oma is nog nooit het land uit **geweest**!
My grandmother has never **been** out of the country!

### 332 - mogelijkheden [n] *possibilities*

In Dubai zijn er veel **mogelijkheden** om werk te vinden.
In Dubai, there are many **possibilities** to find work.

### 333 - aandacht [n] *attention*

Mag ik uw volledige **aandacht** alstublieft, dames en heren.

May I have your full **attention** please, ladies and gentlemen.

### 334 - land [n, v] *land; country, to land ($1^{st}$ and $2^{nd}$ person - present tense)*

Veel mensen vinden Italië een heel mooi **land**.

Many people think Italy is a very beautiful **country**.

### 335 - afgelopen [adj, v] *over; last; past; finished (past participle)*

Heeft u **afgelopen** week overlast gehad van de sneeuwstorm?

Did you experience any inconvenience from the snowstorm **last** week?

### 336 - elk [pron] *every, each*

**Elk** mens is uniek en speciaal!

**Every** person is unique and special!

### 337 - artikel [n] *product for sale; article (journalism/law/grammar)*

Hebben jullie dat **artikel** over Tesla in de krant gelezen?

Have you read that **article** about Tesla in the newspaper?

### 338 - bekend [adj, v] *well-known; familiar; famous; admitted (past participle)*

De zangeres Patricia Paay is heel **bekend** in Nederland.

The singer, Patricia Paay, is very **famous** in The Netherlands.

### 339 - leren [adj, v] *leather; to learn (infinitive and plural subjects - present tense)*

Nederlands **leren** is niet makkelijk, maar ook niet onmogelijk!

**Learning** Dutch isn't easy, but it's not impossible either!

### 340 - zetten [n, v] *push; turn; to put, to place (infinitive and plural subjects - present tense)*

Kom op, we moeten even de tafels en stoelen in de hoek **zetten**.
Come on, we have to **put** the tables and chairs in the corner.

### 341 - klanten [n] *customers*

Een goede marketing-strategie brengt meer **klanten** binnen.
A good marketing strategy brings in more **customers**.

### 342 - denken [n, v] *mind; to think; to believe (infinitive and plural subjects - present tense)*

Wat **denken** je vrienden van je nieuwe partner?
What do your friends **think** about your new partner?

### 343 - ruimte [n] *place; room; space*

Is er **ruimte** in jullie tent voor de hond?
Is there **space** for the dog in your tent?

### 344 - eten [n, v] *food; to eat (infinitive and plural subjects - present tense)*

Mensen in Nederland houden erg van pannenkoeken **eten**!
People in The Netherlands love **eating** pancakes.

### 345 - project [n] *project*

Dit is een interessant **project** om zonnepanelen te promoten.
This is an interesting **project** to promote solar panels.

### 346 - vervolgens [adv] *subsequently, then, afterwards*

Zullen we uit eten gaan en **vervolgens** naar de bioscoop?
Shall we go for dinner and **then** go to the cinema?

### 347 - ieder [pron] *every; each*

Ieder jaar vieren we Bevrijdingsdag op 5 mei.
We celebrate Independence Day on May 5 every year.

### 348 - omgeving [n] *surroundings, area; circle*

Ons huis ligt in een mooie omgeving.
Our house is located in a beautiful area.

### 349 - ziet [v] *to see (2nd and 3rd person - present tense)*

De vogelaar ziet de adelaars meteen.
The birdwatcher immediately sees the eagles.

### 350 - Amsterdam [n] *Amsterdam*

Amsterdam is verreweg de meest populaire stad bij toeristen.
Amsterdam is easily the most popular city for tourists.

### 351 - indien [conj] *in case; if; provided that*

U kunt e-mailen indien u vragen heeft.
You can email in case you have any questions.

### 352 - namelijk [n] *actually; in fact; you see*

Vertrek op tijd, er is namelijk veel verkeer vandaag.
Leave on time: you see, there's a lot of traffic today.

### 353 - ja [adv] *yes*

Ja, kom maar binnen!
Yes, come on in!

### 354 - begin [n, v] *start; to start (1st and 2nd person - present tense)*

Het begin is altijd het moeilijkst!
The start is always the hardest!

**355 - doel** [n, v] *goal; to aim at (1ˢᵗ and 2ⁿᵈ person - present tense)*

Het **doel** van het Rode Kruis is om noodhulp te bieden.
The **goal** of the Red Cross is to offer emergency aid.

**356 - weinig** [n, adj, adv] *little; few*

Er is nog maar **weinig** brood over voor morgen.
There's only **little** bread left for tomorrow.

**357 - beetje** [n] *(a) little (bit)*

Wilt u nog een **beetje** meer water?
Would you like **a little bit** more water?

**358 - hen** [n, pron] *hen; them*

Hebben jullie **hen** al ge-e-maild?
Have you already emailed **them**?

**359 - helpen** [v] *to help (infinitive and plural subjects - present tense)*

De verpleegkundigen **helpen** de patiënten.
The nurses **help** the patients.

**360 - site** [n] *location; website*

Op de **site** van de Rijksoverheid vindt u veel informatie.
On the Central government **website,** you'll find a lot of information.

**361 - zegt** [v] *to say (2ⁿᵈ and 3ʳᵈ person - present tense)*

Men **zegt** vaak dat Nederlanders erg zuinig zijn.
People often **say** Dutch people are very parsimonious.

**362 - stellen** [n, v] *couples; to suppose; to imagine; to*

**put (infinitive and plural subjects - present tense)**

De trainer wil de voetbalspelers op de proef **stellen**.

The trainer wants to **put** the soccer players to the test.

**363 - pas** [n, adv, v] *step; recently; not until; unless; to fit; to try on (1ˢᵗ and 2ⁿᵈ person - present tense)*

De kaaswinkel gaat **pas** om elf uur open.

The cheese store **doesn't** open **until** eleven o'clock.

**364 - daarbij** [adv] *besides; in addition; with that*

Mogen we mayonaise **daarbij**?

Can we have mayonnaise **with that**?

**365 - vorm** [n, v] *form, shape; mold; to shape (1ˢᵗ and 2ⁿᵈ person - present tense)*

Na haar zwangerschap was de danseres weer snel in **vorm**.

After her pregnancy, the dancer quickly got back into **shape**.

**366 - juiste** [adj] *right, correct*

Dat is het **juiste** antwoord!

That's the **correct** answer!

**367 - lijkt** [v] *to seem; to look like (2ⁿᵈ and 3ʳᵈ person - present tense)*

Het **lijkt** morgen beter weer te worden.

It **seems like** the weather will be better tomorrow.

**368 - kans** [n] *chance; opportunity*

Hij maakte geen **kans** in de schaakwedstrijd.

He had no **chance** in the chess competition.

### 369 - ouders [n] *parents*

Mijn **ouders** komen uit Marokko.
My **parents** are from Morocco.

### 370 - team [n] *team*

Welk **team** zal gaan winnen, Ajax of Manchester United?
Which **team** will win, Ajax or Manchester United?

### 371 - januari [n] *January*

Mijn verjaardag is op 16 **januari**.
My birthday is on **January** 16.

### 372 - zaken [n] *business(es); issues; lawsuits*

Nederland en Duitsland doen veel **zaken**.
The Netherlands and Germany do a lot of **business**.

### 373 - enige [pron, n, adj, adv] *the only one; a few; cute; only*

Mevrouw Van Klein is de **enige** tandarts in het dorp.
Mrs. Van Klein is the **only** dentist in the village.

### 374 - langs [prep] *besides; alongside; past*

De kinderen fietsen iedere dag **langs** de supermarkt.
The children cycle **past** the supermarket every day.

### 375 - weken [n, v] *weeks; to soak (infinitive and plural subjects - present tense)*

Over drie **weken** begint mijn vader met zijn nieuwe baan!
In three **weeks,** my dad will start his new job!

### 376 - denk [v] *to think (1st and 2nd person - present*

*tense)*

**Denk** je nog wel eens aan je ex-vriendin?
Do you ever **think** about your ex-girlfriend?

### 377 - boven [n] *above; upstairs*

De slaapkamers zijn **boven** op de tweede verdieping.
The bedrooms are **upstairs** on the second floor.

### 378 - moest [v] *must, to have to (singular subjects - past tense)*

De minister **moest** zijn beleid aan de burgers uitleggen.
The minister **had to** explain his policy to the citizens.

### 379 - ongeveer [adv] *approximately, roughly*

België had in 2016 **ongeveer** elf miljoen inwoners.
Belgium had **approximately** eleven million inhabitants in 2016.

### 380 - vier [num, v] *four; to celebrate (1st and 2nd person - present tense)*

Ik **vier** mijn verjaardag meestal niet.
I usually don't **celebrate** my birthday.

### 381 - hoge [adj] *high; high-pitched*

In België zijn er wat meer **hoge** heuvels dan in Nederland.
In Belgium there are a few more **high** hills than in The Netherlands.

### 382 - gezien [v] *seen (past participle)*

Hebben jullie de nieuwste aflevering van *Goede Tijden, Slechte Tijden* **gezien**?
Have you **seen** the latest *Goede Tijden, Slechte Tijden*? *(longest*

*running Dutch soap-opera)*

### 383 - slechts [adv] *just, only*

Er zijn **slechts** twee middelbare scholen in deze stad.
There are **only** two high schools in this city.

### 384 - juist [adv] *right, correct; just*

Dat wou ik **juist** zeggen!
I **just** wanted to say that!

### 385 - dingen [n] *things*

Blijkbaar is het niet waar dat eksters van glimmende **dingen**
houden!
Apparently, it's not true that magpies like shiny **things**!

### 386 - leuke [adj] *nice; fun; pleasant; funny*

Wat een **leuke** foto's van jou als kind!
Such **nice** photos of you as a child!

### 387 - zoek [adv, v] *missing; to search (1st and 2nd person - present tense)*

Ik **zoek** veel recepten op het Internet.
I **search** for a lot of recipes on the Internet.

### 388 - maart [n] *March*

**Maart** is de derde maand van het jaar.
**March** is the third month of the year.

### 389 - genoeg [pron, conj] *enough; stop!*

Heeft de hond **genoeg** gegeten?
Has the dog eaten **enough**?

**390 - thuis** [n] *(at) home, household*

**Thuis** koken en eten is zeker goedkoper.
Cooking and eating **at home** is definitely cheaper.

**391 - vast** [adj, adv] *steady; permanent; solid; stuck*

Mijn schoenveter zit **vast**, ik krijg 'm er niet uit.
My shoelace is **stuck**, I can't get it out.

**392 - jou** [pron] *you (less common than the other way to say you, which is "je", implies a slight emphasis)*

Ik hou heel veel van **jou**.
I love **you** very much.

**393 - eerder** [adj, adv] *earlier, sooner; previous(ly); preferably*

Sara is meestal **eerder** op het kantoor dan haar collega's.
Sara is usually at the office **earlier** than her coworkers.

**394 - meeste** [n, adj] *(the) most*

Wie heeft de **meeste** boeken bij jou thuis?
Who has **the most** books in your household?

**395 - activiteiten** [n] *activities*

In de zomer zijn er meer **activiteiten** buiten.
In summer there are more outdoor **activities**.

**396 - volledig** [adj, adv] *complete(ly)*

Deze houten vloer is **volledig** verrot.
This wooden floor is **completely** rotten.

**397 - beide** [n, adj] *both*

**Beide** huizen zijn heel mooi, ik zou niet kunnen kiezen.

**Both** houses are very pretty; I wouldn't be able to choose.

### 398 - maanden [n] *months*

De koudste **maanden** in Nederland zijn november tot en met februari.
The coldest **months** in The Netherlands are from November until February.

### 399 - medewerkers [n] *coworkers; employees*

Volgend weekend is het kerstdiner voor alle **medewerkers**.
Next weekend is the Christmas dinner for all **employees**.

### 400 - iedere [adj] *every; each*

Topatleten trainen bijna **iedere** dag.
Professional athletes train almost **every** day.

### 401 - internet [n] *Internet*

Het **internet** wordt steeds belangrijker tegenwoordig.
The **Internet** is becoming more and more important nowadays.

### 402 - lopen [n, v] *gun barrels; to walk; to progress; to flow (infinitive and plural subjects - present tense)*

Langs de grachten **lopen** in Amsterdam is heel ontspannend.
**Walking** along the canals in Amsterdam is very relaxing.

### 403 - problemen [n] *problems; trouble*

Zoonlief, veel plezier op vakantie, maar blijf uit de **problemen**!
My dear son, have fun on your vacation but stay out of **trouble**!

### 404 - samenwerking [n] *collaboration; cooperation*

Hartelijk dank voor onze voorspoedige **samenwerking**.
Thank you very much for our successful **collaboration**.

63

### 405 - voorzien [v] *to provide; to anticipate (infinitive and plural subjects - present tense)*

We **voorzien** geen problemen in dit proces.

We don't **anticipate** any problems in this process.

### 406 - mei [n] *May*

In **mei** gaan we onze hele keuken vervangen.

In **May**, we're going to replace our entire kitchen.

### 407 - minuten [n] *minutes*

Hoeveel **minuten** kan die duiker zijn adem inhouden?

How many **minutes** can that diver hold his breath?

### 408 - plaatsen [n, v] *places; to place, to put (infinitive and plural subjects - present tense)*

Ze gaan het standbeeld in het midden van dit parkje **plaatsen**.

They're going to **place** the statue in the middle of this little park.

### 409 - a [n] *the letter A*

De **A** is de eerste letter van het alfabet.

**A** is the first letter of the alphabet.

### 410 - mogen [v] *may, to be allowed to; to like someone (infinitive and plural subjects - present tense)*

**Mogen** we met onze hond hier naar binnen?

**Are** we **allowed to** enter with our dog here?

### 411 - bovendien [adv] *besides; what's more; not to mention*

Dansen is leuk en ontspannend, en **bovendien** ook nog eens gezond!

Dancing is fun and relaxing, and **not to mention** it's healthy too.

### 412 - verhaal [n] *story*

De lerares leest een **verhaal** voor aan de kinderen.
The teacher reads a **story** to the children.

### 413 - v [n] *the letter V*

Veerle is een mooie naam die met een **v** begint.
Veerle is a nice name that starts with a **V**.

### 414 - zouden [v] *shall; would; will (plural subjects - conditional tense)*

**Zouden** je opa en oma een stukje appeltaart willen?
**Would** your grandpa and grandma like a piece of apple pie?

### 415 - lange [adj] *long, tall*

Het was een **lange** documentaire, maar wel heel interessant.
It was a **long** documentary, but very interesting though.

### 416 - betekent [v] *to mean (2nd and 3rd person - present tense)*

Wat een mooi cadeau, dat **betekent** heel veel voor me!
What a beautiful gift, that **means** a lot to me.

### 417 - blijkt [v] *to seem; to become apparent; to turn out (2nd and 3rd person - present tense)*

Hij **blijkt** zes talen te kunnen spreken!
It **turns out** he can speak six languages!

### 418 - vrij [adj, adv, v] *free (unrestricted); available; fairly; to make love (1st and 2nd person - present tense)*

De nieuwe secretaresse is **vrij** jong, maar erg professioneel.
The new secretary is **fairly** young, but very professional.

### 419 - lezen [v] *to read (infinitive and plural subjects - present tense)*

Leerlingen, kunnen jullie nu alsjeblieft paragraaf acht **lezen**?
Students, can you now please **read** paragraph eight?

### 420 - best [n, adj, adv, interj] *best; quite; "that's fine"*

Mijn zusje is pas negen en ze is al **best** goed in Engels!
My sister is only nine and she's already **quite** good at English!

### 421 - keuze [n] *choice*

Twijfelaars doen er lang over om een simpele **keuze** te maken.
Indecisive people take a long time to make a simple **choice**.

### 422 - ontwikkeling [n] *development; growth*

Vitamines zijn belangrijk voor de **ontwikkeling** van kinderen.
Vitamins are important for children's **development**.

### 423 - gegeven [n, v] *data; topic; given (past participle)*

Hebben jullie je paspoort al aan de receptionist **gegeven**?
Have you already **given** your passport to the receptionist?

### 424 - Jan [n] *the most common first name for Dutch men, John is the equivalent in English*

Hoeveel mensen ken jij die **Jan** heten?
How many people do you know that are called **Jan**?

### 425 - energie [n] *energy*

Het vergt ontzettend veel **energie** om voor kinderen te zorgen.
It takes an incredible amount of **energy** to look after children.

**426 - geheel** [n, adj, adv] *whole; entire(ly)*

De hotelbar wordt **geheel** vernieuwd volgend jaar.
The hotel bar will be **entirely** renovated next year.

**427 - oktober** [n] *October*

In **oktober** zijn er al veel bladeren van de bomen gevallen.
In **October,** a lot of leaves have already fallen off the trees.

**428 - klein** [adj] *small*

Deze peren zijn te **klein** voor het recept.
These pears are too **small** for the recipe.

**429 - september** [n] *September*

In Europa begint de herfst in **september.**
In Europe, fall starts in **September.**

**430 - inmiddels** [adv] *(by) now; so far; in the meantime*

Nederlandse langebaanschaatser Sven Kramer heeft **inmiddels** vier Olympische gouden medailles gewonnen.
Dutch speed skater Sven Kramer has won four Olympic gold medals **so far.**

**431 - lichaam** [n] *body*

Dokter, mijn hele **lichaam** doet zeer.
Doctor, my whole **body** hurts.

**432 - soort** [n] *kind, type*

Gabber is een **soort** techno muziek-ontstaan in Nederland in de jaren negentig.
Gabber is a **kind** of techno music developed in The Netherlands in the nineties.

**433 - kiezen** [n, v] *molar teeth; to choose (infinitive and plural subjects - present tense)*

De klanten konden niet **kiezen** welke van de twee kasten ze wilden kopen.

The customers couldn't **choose** which of the two closets they wanted to buy.

**434 - zoveel** [n] *so much/many; this much/many*

Niet **zoveel** suiker in mijn koffie alsjeblieft; ik ben op dieet.

Not **that much** sugar in my coffee please; I'm on a diet.

**435 - zaterdag** [n] *Saturday*

Aankomende **zaterdag** begint het muziekfestival Pinkpop.

This coming **Saturday**, the music festival Pinkpop will start.

**436 - vrouw** [n] *woman; wife*

Ingrid Baeyens was de eerste Belgische **vrouw** die de top van Mount Everest haalde.

Ingrid Baeyens was the first Belgian **woman** to reach the top of the Mount Everest.

**437 - liggen** [v] *to lie; to be situated (infinitive and plural subjects - present tense)*

De herten **liggen** uit te rusten in het veld.

The deer are **lying** in the field to rest.

**438 - doe** [v] *to do; to function (1st and 2nd person - present tense)*

Ik **doe** drie keer per week aan karate.

I **do** karate three times a week.

### 439 - prachtige [adj] *beautiful, wonderful*

Acda en de Munnik hebben meerdere **prachtige** liedjes geschreven!
Acda and de Munnik wrote several **beautiful** songs!

### 440 - God [n] *God*

Geloof jij in **God**?
Do you believe in **God**?

### 441 - belang [n] *value; relevance; importance*

De verkiezingsuitslag is voor mijn oma niet van **belang**.
The election results don't bear any **importance** for my grandmother.

### 442 - vrouwen [n] *women*

**Vrouwen** verdienen gemiddeld nog steeds minder dan mannen.
**Women** still earn less on average than men.

### 443 - houdt [v] *to hold; to keep; to continue (2^{nd} and 3^{rd} person - present tense)*

Het kindje **houdt** de ballon stevig vast.
The little child is **holding** on tight to the balloon.

### 444 - belangrijke [adj] *important*

De burgemeester heeft morgen een **belangrijke** vergadering.
The mayor has an **important** meeting tomorrow.

### 445 - rol [n] *role; to roll (1^{st} and 2^{nd} person - present tense)*

Voeding speelt een grote **rol** bij het gezond blijven.
Diet plays a big **role** in staying healthy.

69

**446 - stichting** [n] *the founding of; foundation; NGO*

Deze **stichting** vecht voor mensenrechten.

This **NGO** fights for human rights.

**447 - bepaalde** [adj, v] *certain; to determine (singular subjects - past tense)*

**Bepaalde** mensen houden niet van spinnen.

**Certain** people don't like spiders.

**448 - uiteindelijk** [adj, adv] *final(ly); in the end*

Het was lang lopen maar **uiteindelijk** kwamen de wandelaars thuis.

It was a long walk, but **in the end** the hikers got home.

**449 - leden** [n, v] *members; to suffer (plural subjects - past tense)*

We hopen dat alle **leden** van de stichting mee kunnen helpen.

We hope that all **members** of the foundation can collaborate.

**450 - zoeken** [v] *to search (infinitive and plural subjects - present tense)*

Wat **zoeken** jullie precies?

What are you **looking** for exactly?

**451 - ruim** [n, adj, adv] *hold (of a ship); spacious; ample, more than enough*

Jullie zullen **ruim** de tijd hebben om het examen af te maken.

You'll have **ample** time to finish the exam.

**452 - gegevens** [n] *data; (personal) details*

Kunt u hier uw **gegevens** invullen?

Can you fill out your **personal details** here?

**453 - bezig** [adj] *busy*

Hij kon haar niet helpen, want hij was ergens anders mee **bezig**.
He couldn't help her, as he was **busy** doing something else.

**454 - start** [n, v] *start; to start (singular subjects - present tense)*

Als ik de motor **start**, hoor ik een raar geluid.
When I **start** the engine, I hear a weird noise.

**455 - wedstrijd** [n] *competition; race*

Wie heeft de **wedstrijd** gewonnen?
Who won the **competition**?

**456 - muziek** [n] *music*

De tiener vond klassieke **muziek** maar niks.
The teenager didn't like classical **music** at all.

**457 - geleden** [adv, v] *ago; suffered (past participle)*

Heel lang **geleden** in een land hier ver vandaan...
A long time **ago,** in a faraway land...

**458 - dezelfde** [n, adj] *the same*

Je hebt **dezelfde** sportschoenen aan als ik!
You're wearing **the same** sneakers as me!

**459 - tevens** [adv] *also*

Dit is de schrijvers derde en **tevens** zijn laatste boek.
This is the author's third and **also** his last book.

**460 - zorgt** [v] *to look after, to take care of (2nd and 3rd person - present tense)*

De dierenarts **zorgt** voor zieke dieren.

The veterinary **looks after** sick animals.

## 461 - licht [n, adj, adv] *light; slightly; not heavy*

Er is altijd een **licht** aan het eind van de tunnel.
There's always a **light** at the end of the tunnel.

## 462 - vol [adj, adv] *full; entire*

De concertzaal zat helemaal **vol**.
The concert hall was completely **full**.

## 463 - stuk [n, adj] *piece; item; documents; handsome man; broken*

Onze wasmachine is op het moment **stuk**.
Our washing machine is **broken** at the moment.

## 464 - maand [n] *month*

Ga je volgende **maand** een nieuw bed kopen?
Are you going to buy a new bed next **month**?

## 465 - andere [n, adj] *(an)other; different*

Geef jij deze kaarten aan de **andere** spelers?
Will you give these playing cards to the **other** players?

## 466 - ervoor [adv, conj] *in front; for; before; for it/that*

Toen woonden we in Rotterdam, maar **ervoor** woonden we in Breda.
Back then we lived in Rotterdam, but **before** we lived in Breda.

## 467 - korte [adj] *short*

Er zijn nu veel mooie **korte** films online.
There are now a lot of nice **short** films online.

72

**468 - kreeg** [v] *to receive, to get; to obtain (singular subjects - past tense)*

De toerist **kreeg** een gratis kopje koffie in het hotel.
The tourist **got** a free cup of coffee at the hotel.

**469 - probleem** [n] *problem; issue*

Ik doe het wel voor u, geen **probleem**.
I'll do it for you, no **problem**.

**470 - hierbij** [adv] *hereby; with this*

Ik verklaar u **hierbij** tot man en vrouw.
I **hereby** declare you husband and wife.

**471 - daarmee** [adv] *thereby; with that*

Ons personeel helpt u **daarmee**.
Our staff will help you **with that**.

**472 - april** [n] *April*

In **april** loopt mijn werkcontract af.
In **April,** my work contract will end.

**473 - hoog** [adj] *high; tall; distinguished*

Het plafond in dit huis is drie meter **hoog**!
The ceiling in this house is three meters **high**!

**474 - media** [n] *media*

De Koninklijke Familie komt veel in de **media**.
The Royal Family is in the **media** a lot.

**475 - aanwezig** [adj] *present*

Is Meneer Rutte vandaag **aanwezig**?
Is Mr. Rutte **present** today?

**476 - meerdere** [n, pron, adj] *higher placed person; several*

Er lopen **meerdere** rivieren door Nederland.
**Several** rivers run through The Netherlands.

**477 - wijze** [n, adj] *way; wise person; wise*

Onze opa is een hele **wijze** man.
Our grandfather is a very **wise** man.

**478 - november** [n] *November*

In **november** is het meestal al best koud.
In **November,** it's usually quite cold already.

**479 - systeem** [n] *system*

Er wordt binnenkort een nieuw riool**systeem** geïnstalleerd.
A new sewage **system** will be installed soon.

**480 - maak** [v] *to make (1st and 2nd person - present tense)*

**Maak** jij de boterhammen voor morgen?
Will you **make** the sandwiches for tomorrow?

**481 - rekening** [n] *check; (bank) account*

Ober, kunt u alstublieft de **rekening** brengen?
Waiter, could you please bring us the **check**?

**482 - terecht** [adj, adv] *fair, justified; found*

De wrede kritiek was **terecht**. Het was een hele slechte film.
The harsh criticism was **justified**; it was a really bad movie.

**483 - kom** [n, v] *bowl; basin; to come (1st and 2nd person*

*- present tense)*

Ik **kom** niet naar de Nederlandse les morgen.
I'm not **coming** to Dutch class tomorrow.

### 484 - recht [n, adj, adv] *law; right; straight*

Oh jee, dat schilderij hangt niet **recht**!
Oh no, that painting isn't hanging **straight**!

### 485 - meestal [adv] *usually*

De winkels gaan op maandag **meestal** om één uur open.
The stores **usually** open at one o'clock on Mondays.

### 486 - uiteraard [adv] *of course, obviously*

**Uiteraard** is het prima om vragen te stellen.
**Of course,** it's fine to ask questions.

### 487 - meter [n] *meter; indicator; godmother*

Mijn broers zijn beiden meer dan twee **meter** lang!
My brothers are both over two **meters** tall!

### 488 - juni [n] *June*

De zomer begint officieel in **juni**.
Summer officially starts in **June**.

### 489 - delen [n, v] *parts; to divide, to share (infinitive and plural subjects - present tense)*

Zullen we de laatste chocoladereep **delen**?
Shall we **share** the last chocolate bar?

### 490 - februari [n] *February*

Valentijnsdag wordt wereldwijd op veertien **februari** gevierd.
Valentine's Day is celebrated on **February** fourteenth worldwide.

75

**491 - onderwijs** [n, v] *education; teaching; to teach (1ˢᵗ and 2ⁿᵈ person - present tense)*

In het **onderwijs** zijn er altijd banen.
There are always jobs in **education**.

**492 - pagina** [n] *page*

Sla uw boek open op **pagina** vijfendertig.
Open your book at **page** thirty-five.

**493 - persoonlijke** [adj] *personal*

Psychologen beschikken over veel **persoonlijke** informatie.
Psychologists have access to a lot of **personal** information.

**494 - markt** [n] *market; trade*

Groentes zijn het goedkoopst op de wekelijkse **markt**.
Vegetables are cheapest at the weekly **market**.

**495 - toekomst** [n] *future*

Heeft een waarzegger weleens je **toekomst** juist voorspeld?
Has a fortune teller ever predicted your **future** correctly?

**496 - genieten** [v] *to enjoy (infinitive and plural subjects - present tense)*

Van een mooi landschap kan je soms zo **genieten**!
Sometimes you can **enjoy** a beautiful landscape so much!

**497 - advies** [n] *advice*

Een financieel adviseur geeft **advies** over financiële zaken.
A financial advisor offers **advice** about financial issues.

**498 - grootste** [adj] *biggest*

Wat is de **grootste** fout die je ooit hebt gemaakt?

What's the **biggest** mistake you've ever made?

### 499 - wilde [n, adj, v] *wild; to want (singular subjects - past tense)*

Het kleine meisje **wilde** haar groente niet opeten.
The little girl didn't **want** to finish her vegetables.

### 500 - neemt [v] *to take (2nd and 3rd person - present tense)*

**Neemt** u vaak de bus naar het winkelcentrum?
Do you often **take** the bus to the mall?

### 501 - sociale [adj] *social; sociable*

Annabelle is een hele **sociale** meid.
Annabelle is a very **sociable** girl.

### 502 - klant [n] *customer*

Ons motto luidt: de **klant** is koning!
Our motto is: the **customer** is king!

### 503 - stond [v] *to stand; to be written, read (singular subjects - past tense)*

Op het bord **stond**: roken verboden.
The sign **read**: smoking prohibited.

### 504 - mogelijkheid [n] *possibility*

Ze zag geen enkele **mogelijkheid** om de relatie te redden.
She saw no **possibility** of saving the relationship.

### 505 - druk [n, adj, adv, v] *pressure; printed edition; busy, crowded; to push (1st and 2nd person - present tense)*

Haar manager had het altijd super-**druk**.

Her manager was always super **busy**.

## 506 - personen [n] *persons, people*

Kan ik een tafel voor zes **personen** reserveren?
Can I book a table for six **people**?

## 507 - gelukkig [adj, adv] *happy; fortunately*

**Gelukkig** was je hier net op tijd voor de film!
**Fortunately,** you got here just in time for the movie!

## 508 - volgen [v] *to follow (infinitive and plural subjects - present tense)*

Millennials **volgen** vaak heel veel *influencers* op sociale media.
Millennials often **follow** many influencers on social media.

## 509 - voldoende [n. adj, adv,] *passing grade; enough, sufficient*

Ik heb niet **voldoende** gegeten vanochtend.
I haven't eaten **enough** this morning.

## 510 - beeld [n] *statue; image; idea*

Manneken Pis is een heel bekend **beeld** in Brussel.
Manneken Pis is a very famous **statue** located in Brussels.

## 511 - gevoel [n] *feeling; intuition*

De vrouw had het **gevoel** dat ze werd gevolgd.
The woman had the **feeling** that she was being followed.

## 512 - kijk [v] *to look, to watch (1$^{st}$ and 2$^{nd}$ person - present tense)*

**Kijk** jij weleens natuurdocumentaires op tv?
Do you ever **watch** nature documentaries on TV?

### 513 - neem [v] *to take (1st and 2nd person - present tense)*

Ik **neem** soms aspirine als ik hoofdpijn heb.
I sometimes **take** aspirin when I have a headache.

### 514 - periode [n] *period; era*

Deze **periode** van het jaar gaan veel mensen op vakantie.
In this **period** of the year many people go on vacation.

### 515 - december [n] *December*

Op vijf **december** vieren veel families in Nederland en België Sinterklaas.
On the fifth of **December** many families in The Netherlands and Belgium celebrate *Sinterklaas*.

### 516 - product [n] *product (also mathematical)*

Het bedrijf werkt aan een nieuw **product**.
The company is working on a new **product**.

### 517 - huidige [adj] *current; currently*

De effecten van de **huidige** klimaatverandering zijn ernstig.
The effects of the **current** climate change are worrying.

### 518 - waarop [adv] *upon/on/after which*

Hij liet haar schrikken, **waarop** ze flauwviel van de schrik.
He scared her, **upon which** she fainted from the surprise.

### 519 - nieuws [n] *news*

Soms lijkt het alsof er alleen slecht **nieuws** is.
Sometimes it seems as if there's only bad **news**.

### 520 - beschikbaar [adj] *available; in stock; vacant*

Dit product is helaas nu niet **beschikbaar**.
Unfortunately, this product isn't **available** right now.

### 521 - resultaat [n] *result; profits and losses; outcome*

De ontwerper was tevreden over het **resultaat**.
The designer was content with the **result**.

### 522 - geworden [v] *became; got + adjective (past participle)*

Mijn baas was heel boos **geworden,** omdat ik me niet ziek had gemeld.
My boss **got** very **angry,** because I didn't call in sick.

### 523 - opnieuw [adv] *again*

Kan je dat **opnieuw** zeggen alsjeblieft?
Can you say that **again,** please?

### 524 - waarmee [adv] *with which/what; whereby*

**Waarmee** kan de schoonmaakster deze vloer schoonmaken?
**What** can the cleaner clean the floor **with**?

### 525 - grond [n] *ground; land; soil; reason*

Deze akker heeft hele vruchtbare **grond**.
This crop field has very fertile **soil**.

### 526 - hotel [n] *hotel*

Kunt u mij een goedkoop **hotel** in Parijs aanraden?
Could you recommend me a cheap **hotel** in Paris?

### 527 - echte [adj] *real*

Zijn dat de acteurs **echte** tanden?

Are those the actor's **real** teeth?

### 528 - meteen [adv] *immediately, straightaway; at the same time*

Er is brand! We moeten **meteen** evacueren!
There's a fire! We must evacuate **immediately**!

### 529 - plek [n] *place; section; space*

Een moderne televisie neemt niet veel **plek** in.
A modern television set doesn't take up a lot of **space**.

### 530 - heen [adv] *to, towards*

Waar vliegen die meeuwen tijdens de vogeltrek **heen**?
Where do those seagulls fly **to** during their migration?

### 531 - succes [n, interj] *success; "good luck"*

**Succes** met je nieuwe baan!
**Good luck** with your new job!

### 532 - vond [v] *to find; to think (as in opinion) (singular subjects - past tense)*

Wat **vond** je moeder van het cadeautje?
What did your mother **think** of the present?

### 533 - behandeling [n] *treatment; therapy*

De **behandeling** heeft gelukkig gewerkt en de man werd beter.
**Fortunately,** the treatment worked and the man recovered.

### 534 - vijf [num] *five*

Slechts **vijf** leerlingen hebben een voldoende gehaald voor het examen!

Only **five** students achieved the passing grade in the exam!

### 535 - mens [n] *person; human (being)*

De **mens** behoort tot de familie hominidae.
**Humans** belong to the family of Hominidae.

### 536 - voorkomen [n, v] *appearance; to occur; to seem; to prevent (infinitive and plural subjects - present tense) (emphasis differs depending on the meaning)*

Autogordels **voorkomen** veel lichamelijk letsel.
Car seat belts **prevent** a lot of bodily harm.

### 537 - hoogte [n] *height; elevation; level*

De gemiddelde **hoogte** van Nederland is dertig meter boven zeeniveau.
The average **elevation** in The Netherlands is thirty meters above sea level.

### 538 – zon dag [n] *Sunday*

Op **zondag** is de universiteit dicht.
On **Sundays,** the university is closed.

### 539 - vormen [n, v] *shapes; to shape (infinitive and plural subjects in the present tense)*

Vierkanten, cirkels, driehoeken en ovalen zijn de simpelste **vormen**.
Squares, circles, triangles and ovals are the simplest **shapes**.

### 540 - dient [v] *to be used for; to serve; must, ought (2nd and 3rd person in the present tense)*

Men **dient** zich altijd aan de regels te houden.
One **must** always follow the rules.

**541 - geschikt** [adj, v] *appropriate; decent; arranged (past participle)*

Vind je dit een **geschikt** colbert voor het huwelijk?
Do you think this is an **appropriate** suit jacket for the wedding?

**542 - handen** [n] *hands*

Niet vergeten je **handen** te wassen voor het eten.
Don't forget to wash your **hands** before eating.

**543 - helaas** [adv, interj] *unfortunately; (that's) too bad*

**Helaas!** Er zijn geen kaartjes meer beschikbaar.
**Too bad!** There are no more tickets available.

**544 - klaar** [adj] *ready*

Is iedereen in de groep **klaar** om te vertrekken?
Is everyone in the group **ready** to leave?

**545 - t** [n, art, pron] *the letter T; 't is also a common contraction for article and pronoun "het" meaning it*

Had ze **'t** al aan jou gegeven?
Had she already given **it** to you?

**546 - leerlingen** [n] *students*

Hé, waarom zijn er zo weinig **leerlingen** vandaag?
Hey, why are there so few **students** today?

**547 - regelmatig** [adj, adv] *regular(ly)*

De wielrenners trainden **regelmatig**, zelfs in de regen.
The cyclists trained **regularly**, even in the rain.

**548 - sommige** [n, adj] *some; a few*

**Sommige** bomen blijven het hele jaar groen.
**Some** trees stay green the whole year round.

**549 - halen** [v] *to bring; to get; to manage to achieve something (infinitive and plural subjects - present tense)*

Kan jij even de aardbeien uit de keuken **halen**?
Could you **bring** the strawberries from the kitchen?

**550 - hiervoor** [adv] *for this (purpose), before*

Hoeveel betaalde die mevrouw **hiervoor**?
How much did that lady pay **for this**?

**551 - ontvangen** [adv, v] *received; to receive (guests) (infinitive and plural subjects - present tense; past participle)*

Ik heb je berichtje net **ontvangen**.
I've just **received** your message.

**552 - sterk** [adj, adv] *strong; unbelievable*

De wind is heel **sterk** vandaag!
The wind is very **strong** today!

**553 - idee** [n] *idea; notion*

De uitvinder kreeg een **idee** voor een nieuwe uitvinding!
The inventor got an **idea** for a new invention!

**554 - richting** [prep, n] *towards; in the direction of; direction*

Het ziekenhuis is **richting** het vliegveld.

The hospital is **in the direction of** the airport.

### 555 - avond [n] *evening*

Hij drinkt iedere **avond** een glaasje wijn na het eten.
He has a glass of wine after dinner every **evening**.

### 556 - locatie [n] *location*

We zoeken de perfecte **locatie** voor de fotoshoot.
We're looking for the perfect **location** for the photoshoot.

### 557 - opleiding [n] *education; training; course*

Mijn broer heeft zijn **opleiding** aan de universiteit niet afgemaakt.
My brother hasn't finished his university **course**.

### 558 - bijzonder [adj, adv] *special; extraordinary; extremely*

IJsland is een heel **bijzonder** land.
Iceland is a very **special** country.

### 559 - zin [n, v] *sentence; sense; desire; meaning; to like something; to think about something (1st and 2nd person - present tense, slightly archaic)*

Ik heb totaal geen **zin** om de keuken schoon te maken.
I have absolutely no **desire** to clean the kitchen.

### 560 - kant [n] *lace; side*

Aan welke **kant** van de stad ligt het vliegveld?
What **side** of the city is the airport on?

### 561 - valt [v] *to fall (2nd and 3rd person - present tense)*

De acrobaat **valt** bijna nooit tijdens een voorstelling.
The acrobat hardly ever **falls** during a show.

**562 - eind** [n] *end; length*

**Eind** december ga ik een paard kopen!
At the **end** of December, I'm going to buy a horse!

**563 - kort** [adj, adv] *short*

Sorry, maar jouw favoriete t-shirt is nu te **kort**.
Sorry, but your favorite t-shirt is now too **short**.

**564 - heerlijk** [adj, adv] *delicious; wonderful*

De kinderen vonden de pindakaas **heerlijk**.
The children thought the peanut butter was **delicious**.

**565 - woning** [n] *house*

Deze **woning** heeft drie slaapkamers.
This **house** has three bedrooms.

**566 - lid** [n] *member; clause (in law)*

Zijn jullie al **lid** van de bibliotheek?
Are you already a **member** of the library?

**567 - precies** [adj, adv, interj] *exact, precise; exactly*

In Nederland beginnen feestjes meestal **precies** op tijd.
In The Netherlands, parties usually start **exactly** on time.

**568 - hart** [n] *heart*

Je **hart** is één van je belangrijkste organen.
Your **heart** is one of your most important organs.

**569 - centrum** [n] *center*

Alle restaurants en cafeetjes zitten in het **centrum** van de stad.
All the restaurants and cafés are located in the **center** of the city.

### 570 - familie [n] *family*

Voor de vader stond zijn **familie** voorop.
For the father his **family** came first.

### 571 - jong [n, adj] *young*

Midgetgolf is leuk voor iedereen, **jong** en oud.
Mini golf is fun for everyone, **young** and old.

### 572 - s [n] *the letter S*

In veel talen wordt de **s** gebruikt voor het meervoud.
Many languages use **the letter S** for the plural.

### 573 - hierdoor [adv] *because of this; through here*

U poetst uw tanden niet vaak genoeg, **hierdoor** heeft u veel gaatjes.
You're not brushing your teeth often enough, **because of this** you have many cavities.

### 574 - bestaan [v] *to exist (infinitive and plural subjects - present tense)*

Er **bestaan** heel veel soorten insecten.
Many insect species **exist**.

### 575 - stap [n, v] *step; to step (1$^{st}$ and 2$^{nd}$ person - present tense)*

Trouwen is een grote **stap**.
Getting married is a big **step**.

### 576 - ogen [n, v] *eyes; to look (plural subjects - present tense)*

Groene **ogen** komen het minste voor.
Green **eyes** are the least common.

**577 - oplossing** [n] *solution*

Een dijk is een goede **oplossing** tegen overstromingen.
A dike is a good **solution** for floods.

**578 - gehad** [v] *had (past participle)*

De kinderen hebben het heel leuk **gehad**.
The children have **had** a great time.

**579 - derde** [n, adj] *third; third person*

De WC is in de gang, de **derde** deur aan de linkerkant.
The bathroom is in the hallway; the **third** door on the left.

**580 - deelnemers** [n] *participants*

Wat is het maximum aantal **deelnemers** voor deze excursie?
What is the maximum number of **participants** for this excursion?

**581 - beginnen** [v] *to start (infinitive and plural subjects - the present tense)*

De bouwvakkers **beginnen** hun werk om zeven uur 's ochtends.
The laborers **start** their jobs at seven in the morning.

**582 - praktijk** [n] *practice; doctor's practice*

Een goede theorie moet ook in de **praktijk** werken.
A good theory also has to work in **practice**.

**583 - situatie** [n] *situation*

Zijn nicht zat in een moeilijke **situatie** met haar huisbaas.
His cousin was going through a difficult **situation** with her landlord.

**584 - begint** [v] *to start (2<sup>nd</sup> and 3<sup>rd</sup> person - present*

*tense)*

Het bramenseizoen **begint** weer!
The blackberry season is **starting** again!

### 585 - waarvan [adv] *of/from which*

De school had dertig computers, **waarvan** er maar tien werkten.
The school had thirty computers, **of which** only ten worked.

### 586 - x [n] *the letter X*

Niet veel voornamen beginnen met een **x**.
Not many first names start with an **X**.

### 587 - geldt [v] *to apply; to be valid; to be worth (2nd and 3rd person - present tense)*

Deze regel **geldt** voor iedereen!
This rule **applies** to everyone!

### 588 - horen [v] *to hear; to belong (infinitive and plural subjects - present tense)*

Bij de vijver kun je veel kikkers **horen**.
By the pond, you can **hear** a lot of frogs.

### 589 - algemeen [n, adj] *on the whole; general*

Over het **algemeen** eten Nederlanders veel kaas.
In **general**, Dutch people eat a lot of cheese.

### 590 - combinatie [n] *combination*

Je rode schoenen met een gele broek is een gedurfde **combinatie**!
Your red shoes with yellow pants are a bold **combination**!

### 591 - zei [v] *to say (singular subjects - past tense)*

De stewardess **zei** dat we bijna gingen landen.

The stewardess **said** that we were about to land.

## 592 - enkel [n, adj, adv] *ankle; single; solely*

De hockeyspeler kreeg een fikse klap op zijn **enkel**.
The hockey player received a strong blow to his **ankle**.

## 593 - eenvoudig [adj, adv] *simple, easy*

De weg naar het treinstation is heel **eenvoudig**: alleen maar rechtdoor.
The road to the train station is very **simple**: all straight ahead.

## 594 - mannen [n] *men*

In de Tweede Wereldoorlog moesten veel **mannen** het leger in.
In World War Two, many **men** had to join the army.

## 595 - mocht [v] *may, to be allowed to; to like someone (singular subjects - past tense)*

Van mijn ouders **mocht** ik niet alleen naar het feestje.
My parents didn't **allow** me to go to the party alone.

## 596 - totaal [n, adj, adv] *total; totally; entire*

Het **totaal** van de winst in 2019 was teleurstellend.
The **total** of the profit in 2019 was disappointing.

## 597 - betalen [v] *to pay (infinitive and plural subjects - present tense)*

We **betalen** steeds minder met contant geld.
We're **paying** with cash less and less.

## 598 - bezoek [n, v] *visit; the guests; to visit (1st and 2nd*

*person - present tense)*

**Bezoek** je veel musea als je reist?
Do you **visit** a lot of museums when you travel?

### 599 - dienst [n] *work shift; service*

De sociale **dienst** is verantwoordelijk voor het verstrekken van uitkeringen.
Social **services** are responsible for granting social security.

### 600 - reden [n, v] *reason, motive; to ride (plural subjects - past tense)*

Wat was de **reden** voor deze beslissing?
What was the **reason** behind this decision?

### 601 - persoon [n] *person*

Het bedrijf zoekt een extra **persoon** voor het marketing-team.
The company is looking for another **person** for their marketing team.

### 602 - leiden [v] *to lead (infinitive and plural subjects - present tense)*

Alle wegen **leiden** naar Rome.
All roads **lead** to Rome.

### 603 - kleur [n, v] *color; to color (1st and 2nd person - present tense)*

De zee heeft vandaag een hele mooie **kleur**.
The sea has a very beautiful **color** today.

### 604 - kerk [n] *church*

De Nieuwe **Kerk** in Delft is in 1381 gebouwd.
The Nieuwe Kerk (New **Church**) in Delft was built in 1381.

### 605 - woord [n] *word*

In deze zin mist (er) een **woord**.
(A) **word** is missing in this sentence.

### 606 - hoop [n, v] *hope; heap; heaps of (many); to hope (1ˢᵗ and 2ⁿᵈ person - present tense)*

De boer had een hele **hoop** sinaasappels geoogst.
The farmer harvested **heaps of** oranges.

### 607 - actief [adj] *active*

Mijn grootouders zijn nog heel **actief**!
My grandparents are still very **active**!

### 608 - gehouden [v] *held; kept (past participle)*

Er worden veel koeien in deze stal **gehouden**.
A lot of cows are being **kept** in this stable.

### 609 - betreft [v] *to concern (2ⁿᵈ and 3ʳᵈ person - present tense; past participle)*

Wat mij **betreft** kunnen we vandaag vegetarisch eten.
As far as I'm **concerned,** we can eat vegetarian food today.

### 610 - moeilijk [adj, adv] *difficult*

De Nederlandse uitspraak is voor veel buitenlanders best **moeilijk**.
Dutch pronunciation is quite **difficult** for many foreigners.

### 611 - bijzondere [adj] *special; extraordinary; extremely*

De zangeres heeft een hele **bijzondere** stem.
The singer has a very **special** voice.

**612 - km** [n] *km*

Van het noorden naar het zuiden is Nederland ongeveer driehonderd **km** lang.
From north to south, The Netherlands is about three-hundred **km** long.

**613 - moeder** [n] *mother*

Mijn **moeder** heet Agatha en mijn vader Piet.
My **mother**'s name is Agatha and my father's is Piet.

**614 - hoeft** [v] *to have to; to want (2nd and 3rd person - present tense)*

Je **hoeft** niets op te ruimen.
You don't **have to** tidy up anything.

**615 - miljoen** [num] *million*

Ongeveer 27 **miljoen** mensen spreken Nederlands over de hele wereld.
About 27 **million** people speak Dutch worldwide.

**616 - ontstaan** [n, v] *emergence; to originate (infinitive and plural subjects - present tense; past participle)*

Hoe zijn de Alpen **ontstaan**?
How have the Alps **emerged**?

**617 - Europese** [adj] *European*

De **Europese** Unie werd in 1958 gevormd.
The **European** Union was founded in 1958.

**618 - jezelf** [pron] *yourself*

**Jezelf** verwennen mag best!
Pampering **yourself** is absolutely fine!

93

**619 - vrijdag** [n] *Friday*

Mag ik de kamer vanaf **vrijdag** reserveren?
Can I book the room starting from **Friday**?

**620 - kopen** [v] *to buy (infinitive and plural subjects - present tense)*

Waar kan ik een Nederlands woordenboek **kopen**?
Where can I **buy** a Dutch dictionary?

**621 - konden** [v] *can; to be able to (plural subjects - past tense)*

De toeristen **konden** hun gids niet goed verstaan.
The tourists **could** not understand their guide very well.

**622 - waarde** [n] *value*

Ons huis is in **waarde** gedaald.
Our home has has decreased in **value**.

**623 - einde** [n] *end*

Dit is het **einde** van de excursie.
This is the **end** of the excursion.

**624 - nou** [adv, interj] *now (less formal than "nu"); well*

**Nou**, een heel pak koekjes is te veel voor één persoon.
**Well**, a whole box of cookies is too much for one person.

**625 - leveren** [v] *to provide; to deliver; to ship (infinitive and plural subjects - present tense)*

**Leveren** ze de producten ook aan Engeland?
Do they also **ship** the products to England?

**626 - zet** [n, v] *push; turn; to put, to place (singular* *subjects - present tense)*

De vader **zet** de vuilnisbak buiten.
The father **puts** the trash can outside.

### 627 - zichzelf [pron] *oneself; herself; himself; themselves*

De chef had **zichzelf** verbrand tijdens het koken.
The chef had burnt **himself** while cooking.

### 628 - thema [n] *theme; topic*

Wat is het **thema** van de presentatie?
What's the **topic** of the presentation?

### 629 - oud [adj] *old; previous*

Dat brood is **oud**, gooi het maar weg.
That bread is **old**, go ahead and throw it out.

### 630 - boeken [n, v] *books; to book (infinitive and plural subjects - present tense)*

Houd jij ook van de geur van oude **boeken**?
Do you also like the smell of old **books**?

### 631 - natuur [n] *nature*

Wandelen in de **natuur** is stressverlagend.
Walking in **nature** relieves stress.

### 632 - jongeren [n] *young people*

Het Leidseplein is een populaire plek onder **jongeren**.
The Leidseplein is a popular place for **young people**.

### 633 - rijden [v] *to ride; to drive (infinitive and plural*

We **rijden** hier aan de rechterkant.
We **drive** on the right here.

### 634 - gelijk [n, adj, adv] *right; the same*

Oké, je hebt **gelijk**.
Okay, you're **right**.

### 635 - hulp [n] *help; assistant*

De ouders hadden veel **hulp** nodig met hun drieling.
The parents needed a lot of **help** with their triplets.

### 636 - langer [adj, adv] *longer; taller*

Willen jullie nog wat **langer** blijven?
Do you want to stay a little **longer**?

### 637 - risico [n] *risk*

Investeren in aandelen is altijd een **risico**.
Investing in stocks is always a **risk**.

### 638 - procent [n] *percent*

In 2018 had vijftig **procent** van de volwassen Nederlanders
overgewicht.
In 2018, fifty **percent** of Dutch adults were overweight.

### 639 - hoofd [n] *head*

Laten we "**hoofd**, shouders, knie en teen" zingen.
Let's sing "**head**, shoulders, knees and toes".

### 640 - niveau [n] *level*

Het **niveau** van de Olympische Spelen is ontzettend hoog.
The **level** at the Olympics is incredibly high.

### 641 - punten [n] *points*

Het team met de meeste **punten** wint.
The team with the most **points** wins.

### 642 - speciale [adj] *special*

Ik zoek een jurk voor een **speciale** gelegenheid.
I'm looking for a dress for a **special** occasion.

### 643 - kamer [n] *room; chamber*

In de **kamer** stonden een bed, een kast en een bureau.
In the **room** there were a bed, a closet, and a desk.

### 644 - projecten [n] *projects*

De belangrijkste **projecten** worden in december afgerond.
The most important **projects** will be completed in December.

### 645 - regio [n] *region; area*

In mijn **regio** wordt veel mais geteeld.
In my **region,** a lot of corn is cultivated.

### 646 - geplaatst [v] *placed, put (past participle)*

Het bedrijf had een advertentie in de krant **geplaatst**.
The company **put** an advert in the newspaper.

### 647 - d [n] *the letter D*

Eindigt dit woord met een **d** of een t?
Does this word end in a **D** or a T?

### 648 - kracht [n] *power; strength*

Bodybuilders hebben veel **kracht**.
Bodybuilders have a lot of **strength**.

**649 - plan** [n, v] *plan; map; to plan (1st and 2nd person - present tense)*

Wat is het **plan** voor het weekend?
What's the **plan** for the weekend?

**650 - ervaren** [adj, v] *experienced; to experience (infinitive and plural subjects - present tense; past participle)*

Onze geschiedenisleraar is ontzettend **ervaren**.
Our history teacher is incredibly **experienced**.

**651 - rust** [n, v] *rest; quiet; to rest (singular subjects - present tense)*

De manager kreeg doordeweeks niet genoeg **rust**.
The manager didn't get enough **rest** during the week.

**652 - o.a.** [adv] *abbreviation for "onder andere" meaning among other things; e.g.*

Qua warme dranken hebben we **o.a.** thee, koffie en warme chocolademelk.
For hot drinks we have tea, coffee, and hot chocolate, **amongst others**.

**653 - financiële** [adj] *financial*

De gokverslaafde had ernstige **financiële** problemen.
The gambling addict had severe **financial** problems.

**654 - schrijven** [n, v] *letter, to write (infinitive and plural subjects - present tense)*

**Schrijven** jullie allemaal iets leuks op de kaart?
Will you all **write** something nice on the postcard?

### 655 - juli [n] *July*

In **juli** begint de schoolvakantie.
School holidays will start in **July**.

### 656 - genomen [v] *taken (past participle)*

Heeft u weleens de veerboot naar het eiland Texel **genomen**?
Have you ever **taken** the ferry to the island of Texel?

### 657 - bestaande [adj] *existing*

Ondanks de bedrijfsfusie zullen **bestaande** contracten behouden worden.
Despite the company merger, **existing** contracts will be maintained.

### 658 - training [n] *training; course*

Vandaag was de **training** extra moeilijk!
Today's **training** was extra tough!

### 659 - diensten [n] *services*

Ons mediabedrijf biedt verscheidene **diensten** aan.
Our media company offers several **services**.

### 660 - allerlei [adj] *all sorts of*

Op vlooienmarkten worden **allerlei** spullen verkocht.
At flea markets, **all sorts** of things are sold.

### 661 - krijg [v] *to receive, to get; to obtain (1st and 2nd person - present tense)*

**Krijg** jij weleens handgeschreven brieven?
Do you ever **receive** handwritten letters?

**662 - wensen** [n, v] *wishes; to wish (infinitive and plural subjects - present tense)*

Wij **wensen** u fijne kerstdagen en een gelukkig nieuwjaar!
We **wish** you a Merry Christmas and a Happy New Year.

**663 - klik** [n, v] *click; to click; to reveal secrets (1<sup>st</sup> and 2<sup>nd</sup> person - present tense)*

Als ik op dit knopje **klik**, sluit het programma af.
When I **click** this button, the program closes.

**664 - kwamen** [v] *to come (plural subjects - past tense)*

Wanneer **kwamen** er voor het eerst Indonesiërs naar Nederland?
When did Indonesians first **come** to The Netherlands?

**665 - ontwikkelen** [v] *to develop (infinitive and plural subjects - present tense)*

We **ontwikkelen** steeds complexere computerprogramma's.
We're **developing** more and more complex computer programs.

**666 - wist** [v] *to know (singular subjects - past tense)*

Zelfs de leraar **wist** het antwoord niet.
Even the teacher didn't **know** the answer.

**667 - algemene** [adj] *general*

Klik hier om de **algemene** voorwaarden te lezen.
Click here to read our **general** terms and conditions.

**668 - vakantie** [n] *holidays; vacation*

Hoe was jullie **vakantie** in Rusland?
How was your **vacation** in Russia?

**669 - woorden** [n] *words*

Veel Duitse en Nederlandse **woorden** lijken erg op elkaar.
Many German and Dutch **words** are very similar.

**670 - daardoor** [adv] *because of that; that's why*

Hij was begonnen met hardlopen, **daardoor** was hij zoveel afgevallen.
He took up running, **that's why** he had lost so much weight.

**671 - organisaties** [n] *organizations*

Welke **organisaties** werken er met re-integratie van ex-gevangenen?
Which **organizations** are working on reintegrating ex-convicts?

**672 - belangrijkste** [adj] *most important*

Dit zijn de **belangrijkste** regels in onze fabriek.
These are the **most important** rules in our factory.

**673 - onderdeel** [n] *part*

Er mist een **onderdeel** van de motor.
A **part** of the engine is missing.

**674 - hetzelfde** [n, adj] *the same*

De tweeling had **hetzelfde** hoedje op.
The twins were wearing **the same** hat.

**675 - vrienden** [n] *friends*

Veel van hun **vrienden** wonen in het buitenland.
Many of their **friends** live abroad.

**676 - loopt** [v] *to walk; to function (2ⁿᵈ and 3ʳᵈ person -*

*present tense)*

Kijk, daar **loopt** een wolf!
Look, there's a wolf **walking** over there!

### 677 - wonen [v] *to live (infinitive and plural subjects - present tense)*

Veel families **wonen** in de nieuwe wijk.
A lot of families **are living** in the new neighborhood.

### 678 - hard [adj, adv] *hard; tough; harsh; fast*

De sprinter rende heel **hard**.
The sprinter ran very **fast**.

### 679 - vader [n] *father*

Haar **vader** werkt voor de regering.
Her **father** is working for the government.

### 680 - augustus [n] *August*

Mijn favoriete maand van het jaar is **augustus**.
My favorite month of the year is **August**.

### 681 - service [n] *service*

Dit restaurant bood hele goede **service**.
This restaurant offered very good **service**.

### 682 - gevallen [n, v] *cases, fallen (past participle)*

Iedereen is weleens van een schommel **gevallen**.
Everyone has **fallen** off a swing once.

### 683 - resultaten [n] *results*

De **resultaten** van het team waren teleurstellend.
The **results** of the team were disappointing.

**684 - voordat** [conj] *before*

Ga je douchen **voordat** we uit eten gaan?
Are you going to have a shower **before** we go out for dinner?

**685 - partijen** [n] *(political) parties; matches*

Hoeveel politieke **partijen** zijn er in jouw land?
How many political **parties** are there in your country?

**686 - immers** [adv] *indeed; after all*

Fouten maken is niet erg, je bent **immers** nog aan het leren.
Making mistakes is no problem; **after all**, you're still learning.

**687 - landen** [n, v] *countries; to land (infinitive and plural subjects - present tense)*

Hoeveel **landen** zijn er nu lid van de Europese Unie?
How many **countries** are now members of the European Union?

**688 - begon** [v] *to start (singular subjects - past tense)*

Net toen we vertrokken, **begon** het heel hard te regenen.
It **started** to pour with rain just as we left.

**689 - maakte** [v] *to make (singular subjects - past tense)*

De artiest **maakte** ongelofelijk mooie armbanden.
The artist **made** incredibly beautiful bracelets.

**690 - prima** [adj, adv] *excellent; fine*

Dat is **prima**, ik kom morgen om acht uur terug.
That's **fine**, I'll come back tomorrow at eight o'clock.

**691 - vereniging** [n] *association; reunion*

Een **vereniging** mag geen winst maken.

103

An **association** isn't allowed to make a profit.

**692 - prijzen** [n, v] *prices; prizes; to price; to praise (infinitive and plural subjects - present tense)*

De **prijzen** zijn recentelijk veel gestegen.
**Prices** have recently gone up a lot.

**693 - daarvoor** [adv, conj] *in front of; before; for that*

Heel erg lief dat jullie me geholpen hebben, bedankt **daarvoor**.
Very sweet of you to have helped me, thanks **for that**.

**694 - bezoekers** [n] *visitors*

Natuurgebieden trekken steeds meer **bezoekers** aan.
Natural areas are attracting more and more **visitors**.

**695 - nadat** [conj] *after (which)*

Het werd snel koud **nadat** de zon was ondergegaan.
It got cold quickly **after** the sun had set.

**696 - kennen** [v] *to know (infinitive and plural subjects - present tense)*

**Kennen** jullie het werk van de schilder Rembrandt?
Do you **know** the work of the painter Rembrandt?

**697 - vroeg** [adj, v] *early; to ask (singular subjects - past tense)*

Bakkers beginnen heel **vroeg** met hun werk.
Bakers start their job very **early**.

**698 - vanwege** [prep] *because of; due to*

De elektriciteit is uitgevallen **vanwege** de hevige storm.
There was a power cut **due to** the heavy storm.

**699 - komende** [adj] *coming*

De **komende** maanden wordt het heel koud.
In the **coming** months, it's going to be very cold.

**700 - top** [n, adj, interj] *peak; management; great*

Oh, dus je kan me morgen helpen met verhuizen? **Top!**
Oh, so you can help me move tomorrow? **Great!**

**701 - zag** [v] *to see (singular subjects - past tense)*

**Zag** jij die vallende ster ook?
Did you **see** that shooting star too?

**702 - middel** [n] *waist; medication; means*

De broek zit te strak rond zijn **middel**.
The pants are too tight around his **waist**.

**703 - spel** [n, v] *game; to spell (singular subjects - past tense)*

Yahtzee is een **spel** met dobbelstenen.
Yahtzee is a **game** with dice.

**704 - betrokken** [adj, v] *sad; involved; to involve (plural subjects - past tense; past participle)*

Er waren veel politici bij het schandaal **betrokken**.
Many politicians were **involved** in the scandal.

**705 - genoemd** [adj, v] *mentioned; called (past participle)*

Ik heet Elisabeth, maar word meestal Ellie **genoemd**.
My name is Elisabeth, but am usually **called** Ellie.

**706 - gevonden** [v] *found (past participle)*

De archeologen hebben een nieuwe tempel **gevonden**.
The archaeologists have **found** a new temple.

**707 - Europa** [n] *Europe*

**Europa** ligt ten noorden van Afrika.
**Europe** lies north of Africa.

**708 - film** [n, v] *film; movie; to film (1$^{st}$ and 2$^{nd}$ person - present tense)*

De Nederlandse **film** Ciske de Rat had heel veel succes.
The Dutch **movie** *Ciske de Rat* was very successful.

**709 - ooit** [adv] *at some point; ever*

Heeft u **ooit** een bloedtransfusie ontvangen?
Have you **ever** received a blood transfusion?

**710 - voorbeeld** [n] *example*

Bekijk het **voorbeeld** en maak de oefening af.
Look at the **example** and finish the exercise.

**711 - raad** [n, v] *advice; council; to guess (1$^{st}$ and 2$^{nd}$ person - present tense)*

**Raad** eens wat we vanavond eten!
**Guess** what we're going to eat tonight!

**712 - stelt** [n, v] *stilt; to suppose; to imagine; to put (2$^{nd}$ and 3$^{rd}$ person - present tense)*

Jouw berichtje **stelt** me gerust.
Your message **puts** me at ease.

### 713 - huid [n] *skin; hide*

Baby**huid** is veel gevoeliger.
Baby **skin** is much more sensitive.

### 714 - etc [adv] *etc. (et cetera)*

Mijn moeder is dol op zoet: chocolade, taart, koekjes, **etc.**
My mother loves sweet things: chocolate, pie, cookies, **etc.**

### 715 - speciaal [adj] *special*

We hebben een **speciaal** liedje voor onze ouders geschreven.
We wrote a **special** song for our parents.

### 716 - gebracht [v] *brought; took (past participle)*

Ze hebben jullie naar het vliegveld **gebracht.**
They **took** you to the airport.

### 717 - tuin [n] *garden*

Dit is de mooiste **tuin** in de straat.
This is the prettiest **garden** in the street.

### 718 - antwoord [n, v] *answer, to answer (1ˢᵗ and 2ⁿᵈ person - present tense)*

Dat is helaas het verkeerde **antwoord**, ben ik bang.
Unfortunately, that's the wrong **answer**, I'm afraid.

### 719 - leggen [v] *to lay, to put (infinitive and plural subjects - present tense)*

Vergeet niet de schone was in de kast te **leggen**!
Don't forget to **put** the clean laundry in the closet!

### 720 - vorige [adj] *former; previous*

**Vorige** maand heeft mijn vrouw promotie gekregen.

**Last** month my wife got a promotion.

### 721 - hoger [adj, adv] *higher*

Deze boom is **hoger** dan die andere.
This tree is **higher** than the other one.

### 722 - gekomen [v] *come (past participle)*

Wie is er nog meer naar het feestje **gekomen**?
Who else has **come** to the party?

### 723 - afhankelijk [adj] *dependent*

We zijn erg **afhankelijk** geworden van het internet.
We've become quite **dependent** on the Internet.

### 724 - feit [n] *fact*

Dat is geen **feit**, het is een mening.
That's not a **fact**, it's an opinion.

### 725 - gebeurt [v] *to happen (2$^{nd}$ and 3$^{rd}$ person - present tense)*

Een ongeluk in huis **gebeurt** snel.
An accident in the home **happens** quickly.

### 726 - welkom [n, adj, interj] *welcome*

**Welkom** thuis!
**Welcome** back home!

### 727 - soorten [n] *types; species*

Er zijn veel **soorten** vogels op de Wadden.
There are many **species** of birds on the Wadden.

### 728 - bestuur [n, v] *management; to drive; to manage*

*(1st and 2nd person – present tense)*

Het **bestuur** besloo bezuinigingen door te voeren.
**Management** decided to introduce budget cuts.

### 729 - wet [n] *law*

De nieuwe **wet** gaat per 1 januari in.
The new **law** goes into effect on January first.

### 730 - tekst [n] *text; lyrics*

Lees de **tekst** en beantwoord de vragen.
Read the **text** and answer the questions.

### 731 - e [n] *the letter E*

Eloise is een mooie naam die met een **e** begint.
Eloise is a nice name starting with an **E**.

### 732 - z [n] *the letter Z*

De **z** is de laatste letter van het alfabet.
**Z** is the last letter of the alphabet.

### 733 - actie [n] *action; campaign*

We moeten **actie** ondernemen tegen klimaatverandering.
We must take **action** against climate change.

### 734 - ervan [adv] *of it/that*

Dat is het mooie **ervan**!
That's the nice part **of it**!

### 735 - overheid [n] *government*

De **overheid** heft belastingen om te regeren.
The **government** levies taxes in order to govern.

### 736 - stand [n] *position; class; stall; score*

Wat is de **stand** van de wedstrijd?
What's the **score** of the game?

### 737 - kleuren [n, v] *colors; to color (infinitive and plural subjects - present tense)*

Die twee **kleuren** staan mooi bij elkaar.
Those two **colors** look good together.

### 738 - volgt [v] *to follow (2^{nd} and 3^{rd} person - present tense)*

De politie **volgt** de overvallers.
The police is **following** the robbers.

### 739 - proberen [v] *to try (infinitive and plural subjects - present tense)*

Willen jullie deze pindakaas **proberen**?
Do you want to **try** this peanut butter?

### 740 - bouwen [v] *to build (infinitive and plural subjects - present tense)*

De regering is hier een nieuwe school aan het **bouwen**.
The government is **building** a new school here.

### 741 - gevolg [n] *consequence; following*

Soms kan een kleine daad een enorm **gevolg** hebben
Sometimes a small act can have an enormous **consequence**.

### 742 - liefde [n] *love*

Veel gedichten gaan over **liefde**.
Many poems are about **love**.

**743 - opdracht** [n] *assignment; command*

De kinderen gaan de **opdracht** samen doen.
The children will do the **assignment** together.

**744 - half** [n, adj, adv] *half*

De student had de uitleg maar **half** begrepen.
The student had only **half** understood the explanation.

**745 - waarschijnlijk** [adj, adv] *likely; probably*

Samantha komt **waarschijnlijk** weer te laat.
Samantha is **probably** going to be late again.

**746 - deed** [v] *to do (singular subjects - past tense)*

Wat **deed** Reinout Oerlemans voordat hij filmregisseur werd?
What **did** Reinout Oerlemans **do** before he became a movie director?

**747 - blij** [adj, adv] *happy*

Zijn ze **blij** dat ze geslaagd zijn?
Are they **happy** they've graduated?

**748 - standaard** [n, adj, adv] *stand; standard*

Zet je je fiets in de **standaard**?
Will you put your bicycle in the **stand**?

**749 - publiek** [n, adj, adv] *audience; public*

Het **publiek** gaf de band een staande ovatie.
The **audience** gave the band a standing ovation.

**750 - seizoen** [n] *season*

In welk **seizoen** komen hier de meeste toeristen?
In which **season** do the most tourists come here?

**751 - bereiken** [v] *to achieve; to contact (infinitive and plural subjects - past tense)*

Jullie kunnen me op mijn mobiele nummer **bereiken**.

You can **contact** me on my mobile phone.

**752 - kaart** [n, v] *map; menu; (post)card; to play cards (singular subjects - present tense)*

Ober, heeft u eventueel een **kaart** in het Engels?

Waiter, do you perhaps have a **menu** in English?

**753 - bepaald** [adj, adv, v] *certain; certainly; determined (past participle)*

Heeft u een **bepaald** beeld van uw droomhuis?

Do you have a **certain** image of your dream house?

**754 - uitgevoerd** [v] *exported; carried out; performed (past participle)*

Het computerprogramma heeft de instructies correct **uitgevoerd**.

The computer program has **carried out** the instructions correctly.

**755 - hiermee** [adv] *with this*

Wat denk je dat de schrijver **hiermee** bedoelt?

What do you think the writer means **with this**?

**756 - gesprek** [n] *conversation*

De schrijver had een interessant **gesprek** met de journalist.

The writer had an interesting **conversation** with the journalist.

**757 - nee** [n, interj] *no*

**Nee**, we willen geen spruitjes.

**No**, we don't want any sprouts.

### 758 - Rotterdam [n] *Rotterdam*

**Rotterdam** had in 2018 zeshonderdveertigduizend inwoners.
**Rotterdam** had six hundred and forty thousand inhabitants in 2018.

### 759 - functie [n] *function; job*

Het advocatenkantoor heeft een vacature voor een **functie**.
The law firm has a **job** opening.

### 760 - dankzij [prep] *thanks to*

**Dankzij** de studiebeurs kon het meisje haar studie betalen.
**Thanks to** the educational grant, the girl was able to pay for her studies.

### 761 - bedrag [n] *amount*

Weet u zeker dat het **bedrag** klopt?
Are you sure the **amount** is correct?

### 762 - gesteld [v] *to like someone; posed (a question) (past participle)*

Zij was erg op haar nichtje **gesteld**.
She **liked** her cousin a lot.

### 763 - maat [n] *mate, friend (informal); size*

Deze **maat** past niet.
This **size** doesn't fit.

### 764 - makkelijk [adj, adv] *easy*

Binnen Europa reizen is **makkelijk**.
Traveling within Europe is **easy**.

### 765 - centraal [adj, adv] *central; crucial*

Het treinstation Amsterdam **Centraal** is een iconische plek.
Amsterdam **Central** train station is an iconic place.

### 766 - nummer [n] *number; issue, song*

Veel liedjes van de band Doe Maar werden **nummer** één.
Many songs by the band Doe Maar reached **number** one.

### 767 - eeuw [n] *century; long time*

De zeventiende eeuw staat in Nederland bekend als de Gouden **Eeuw**.
The seventeenth century in The Netherlands is known as the Golden **Age**.

### 768 - gekozen [adj, v] *chosen (past participle)*

Onze zoon heeft het adoptiehondje zelf **gekozen**.
Our son has **chosen** the adoption dog himself.

### 769 - speelt [v] *to play (an instrument); (2nd and 3rd person - present tense)*

Uw collega **speelt** de trompet, toch?
Your coworker **plays** the trumpet, right?

### 770 - vaste [adj] *steady; permanent; solid*

We hebben al tien jaar een **vaste** relatie.
We've been in a **steady** relationship for ten years now.

### 771 - maandag [n] *Monday*

De meeste mensen werken van **maandag** tot en met vrijdag.
Most people work from **Monday** to Friday.

### 772 - brengt [v] *to bring (2nd and 3rd person - present*

*tense)*

Mijn broer **brengt** altijd souvenirs terug van zijn reizen.
My brother always **brings** back souvenirs from his travels.

### 773 - ontwikkeld [adj, v] *developed (past participle)*

De plant was volledig **ontwikkeld**.
The plant has **developed** completely.

### 774 - vallen [n, v] *traps; to fall (infinitive and plural subjects - present tense)*

Bij het skateboarden is het normaal om vaak te **vallen**.
When skateboarding, it's normal to **fall** a lot.

### 775 - hoewel [conj] *although*

**Hoewel** ik al veel gelopen heb vandaag, ben ik nog niet moe.
**Although** I've already walked a lot today, I'm still not tired.

### 776 - reis [n, v] *journey; to travel (1ˢᵗ and 2ⁿᵈ person - present tense)*

Hoe lang duurt de **reis**?
How long does the **journey take**?

### 777 - gelegen [adj, adv, v] *convenient; located (past participle)*

Komt het **gelegen**?
Is this a **convenient** time?

### 778 - tien [num] *ten*

De peuter kan al tot **tien** tellen.
The toddler can already count to **ten**.

### 779 - Google [n] *Google*

**Google** is al jarenlang de populairste zoekmachine.
**Google** has been the most popular search engine for years.

### 780 - voorwaarden [n] *conditions*

Wat zijn de **voorwaarden** van de overeenkomst?
What are the **conditions** of the agreement?

### 781 - ondanks [prep] *despite*

**Ondanks** de regen zijn we toch gaan voetballen.
**Despite** the rain, we went to play soccer anyway.

### 782 - wachten [v] *to wait (infinitive and plural subjects - present tense)*

Jullie moeten hier even **wachten**.
You have to **wait** here for a moment.

### 783 - prachtig [adj, adv] *beautiful(ly), marvelous(ly)*

Het kinderkoor zong **prachtig**.
The children's choir sang **beautifully**.

### 784 - voeren [v] *to feed (infinitive and plural subjects - present tense)*

Wie gaat vandaag de konijnen **voeren**?
Who's going to **feed** the rabbits today?

### 785 - Utrecht [n] *Utrecht (city)*

In **Utrecht** wonen meer dan dertigduizend studenten.
In **Utrecht,** there are over thirty thousand students.

### 786 - internationale [adj] *international*

Op de Universiteit in Wageningen zijn veel **internationale** studenten.
At Wageningen University there are many **international** students.

### 787 - name [n] *archaic form of naam (name), mostly used in set expressions*

Tom houdt van Latijns-Amerikaanse muziek, **met name** salsa.
Tom likes Latin-American music, **especially** salsa.

### 788 - unieke [adj] *unique*

Het sjieke huis had **unieke** meubels.
The posh house had **unique** furniture.

### 789 - links [n, adj] *left-handed; on the left; (website) links*

De badkamer is de tweede deur **links**.
The bathroom is the second door **on the left**.

### 790 - bleek [adj, adv, v] *pale; to turn out; to seem (singular subjects - past tense)*

Het **bleek** niet nodig te zijn.
It **turned out** not to be necessary.

### 791 - inclusief [adv] *inclusive; including*

Is deze prijs **inclusief** BTW?
Is this the cost **including** sales taxes?

### 792 - studenten [n] *students*

In deze studentenflat wonen acht **studenten**.
Eight **students** are living in this student's apartment.

### 793 - daarvan [adv] *of that*

Die taart is voor morgen, niets **daarvan** pakken!
That cake is for tomorrow, don't take any **of that**!

### 794 - inhoud [n] *content(s); volume; index*

Dit opstel heeft totaal geen **inhoud**.
This essay totally lacks **content**.

### 795 - zat [adj, v] *drunk; fed up; to sit (singular subjects - past tense)*

Mijn moeder was mijn rommel **zat**.
My mother was **fed up** with my clutter.

### 796 - ver [adj, adv] *far*

Het winkelcentrum is te **ver** om heen te lopen.
The shopping mall is too **far** to walk to.

### 797 - bekijken [v] *to view; to examine; to consider (infinitive and plural subjects - present tense)*

Laten we dit schilderij van dichtbij **bekijken**.
Let's **examine** this painting closely.

### 798 - collega [n] *coworker*

Ik ga vrijdag uit eten met mijn **collega** Luuk.
I'm going out for dinner on Friday with my **coworker** Luuk.

### 799 - communicatie [n] *communication*

Door het internet is **communicatie** nu razendsnel.
Due to the Internet, **communication** is now superfast.

**800 - o** [n] *the letter O*

Is dit een **o** of een nul?
Is this the letter **O** or a zero?

**801 - kent** [v] *to know (2^{nd} and 3^{rd} person - present tense)*

**Kent** zij de Belgische band K's Choice?
Does she **know** the Belgian band K's Choice?

**802 - los** [adj, adv, v] *loose; independent; to unload; to shoot (1^{st} and 2^{nd} person - present tense)*

Dit touw zit te **los**.
This rope is too **loose**.

**803 - dieren** [n] *animals*

Dolfijnen zijn zulke prachtige **dieren**.
Dolphins are such beautiful **animals**.

**804 - cm** [n] *cm*

De tafel is 145 bij 110 **cm**.
The table is 145 by 110 **cm**.

**805 - begeleiding** [n] *accompaniment; guidance; counseling; supervision*

De leerlingen met een achterstand krijgen extra **begeleiding**.
Students that are behind receive extra **counseling**.

**806 - bekende** [n, adj] *acquaintance; well-known; familiar; famous*

André van Duin is een heel **bekende** televisiepresentator.
André van Duin is a very **well-known** television presenter.

**807 - zon** [n, v] *sun; to sunbathe (1<sup>st</sup> and 2<sup>nd</sup> person - present tense)*

In de winter is er veel minder **zon**.
In winter, there is much less **sun**.

**808 - hieronder** [adv] *below; following this*

De uitleg staat **hieronder**.
The explanation is written **below**.

**809 - donderdag** [n] *Thursday*

Aankomende **donderdag** is haar mans verjaardag.
This **Thursday** is her husband's birthday.

**810 - begonnen** [v] *to start (plural subjects - past tense; past participle)*

De scholen zijn weer **begonnen**.
Schools have **started** classes again.

**811 - lokale** [adj] *local*

Je kan het beste groenten kopen van **lokale** boeren.
It's best if you buy vegetables from **local** farmers.

**812 - dagelijks** [adj, adv] *daily*

Het afval wordt **dagelijks** opgehaald.
The waste is picked up **daily**.

**813 - slag** [n] *hit; beat; stroke; battle;*

De **Slag** aan de Somme vond plaats tijdens de Eerste Wereldoorlog.
The **Battle** of the Somme occurred during the First World War.

### 814 - gericht [adj, adv, v] *focused; aimed (past participle)*

De manager was voornamelijk **gericht** op resultaten behalen.
The manager mainly **focused** on achieving results.

### 815 - reactie [n] *reaction*

Wat was de **reactie** van jullie ouders op het nieuws?
What was your parents' **reaction** to the news?

### 816 - cursus [n] *course*

Mijn zus wil een **cursus** creatief schrijven gaan volgen.
My sister would like to take a **course** in creative writing.

### 817 - vertellen [v] *to tell; to count incorrectly (infinitive and plural subjects - present tense)*

De lerares gaat een verhaal over kaboutertjes **vertellen**.
The teacher is going to **tell** a story about little gnomes.

### 818 - helft [n] *half*

Zullen we ieder de **helft** betalen?
Shall we each pay **half**?

### 819 - leeftijd [n] *age*

De actrice probeerde haar **leeftijd** geheim te houden.
The actress tried to keep her **age** a secret.

### 820 - materiaal [n] *material*

Deze tent is van regenbestendig **materiaal** gemaakt.
This tent is made of rainproof **material**.

### 821 - doordat [conj] *because (of)*

**Doordat** je zoveel tijd had, kon je de trui snel afbreien.

**Because** you had so much time, you could finish knitting the sweater quickly.

### 822 - gemakkelijk [adj, adv] *easy(ly); comfortable, comfortably*

Nederlands leren is niet **gemakkelijk**.
Learning Dutch isn't **easy**.

### 823 - b [n] *the letter B*

De **b** is voor beer.
**The letter B** is for bear.

### 824 - relatie [n] *relationship*

De man had een goede **relatie** met zijn schoonmoeder.
The man had a good **relationship** with his mother-in-law.

### 825 - geschiedenis [n] *history*

De **geschiedenis** van de Romeinen is heel interessant.
The **history** of the Romans is very interesting.

### 826 - Nederlands [n, adj] *Dutch, used to refer to the Dutch language, nationality, and its citizens*

Een biertje drinken op een caféterras is typisch **Nederlands**.
Drinking a beer on a café terrace is typically **Dutch**.

### 827 - ondersteuning [n] *support; assistance*

Het IT-bedrijf biedt uitstekende technische **ondersteuning**.
The IT company offers excellent technical **support**.

### 828 - opgenomen [adj, v] *recorded; incorporated; answered the phone; hospitalized (past participle)*

De camera's hebben het hele programma **opgenomen**.

The cameras have **recorded** the entire show.

### 829 - aanbod [n] *offer; supply*

De verkoper accepteert het **aanbod**.
The seller accepts the **offer**.

### 830 - én [conj] *and (like "en", but the accent indicates special emphasis)*

Ze willen een video **én** foto's van hun bruiloft.
They want a video *and* photos of their wedding.

### 831 - tips [n] *tips*

Heb je **tips** om mijn Nederlands te verbeteren?
Do you have any **tips** to improve my Dutch?

### 832 - rode [n, adj] *red*

Jouw vriendin Roxanne heeft een **rode** jurk aan.
Your friend Roxanne is wearing a **red** dress.

### 833 - proces [n] *process; lawsuit*

Een scheiding is een pijnlijk **proces**.
A divorce is a painful **process**.

### 834 - groene [n, adj] *green*

Een **groene** omgeving is gezond.
A **green** environment is healthy.

### 835 - midden [n, adv] *(the) middle*

De markt is in het **midden** van de stad.
The market is in the **middle** of the city.

### 836 - sport [n, v] *sport; to play a sport (singular subjects*

*- present tense)*

Welke **sport** spelen jullie?
What **sport** do you play?

### 837 - gedurende [prep] *during*

Janet viel **gedurende** de documentaire in slaap.
Janet fell asleep **during** the documentary.

### 838 - gingen [v] *to go (plural subjects - past tense)*

De schapen **gingen** samen naar de wei.
The sheep **went** to the meadow together.

### 839 - rest [n, v] *rest; to remain (singular subjects - present tense, slightly archaic)*

We hebben de **rest** van de week vakantie.
We're on holidays the **rest** of the week.

### 840 - bank [n] *bank; sofa; bench*

Deze leren **bank** is nu in de aanbieding.
This leather **sofa** is now discounted.

### 841 - specifieke [adj, adv] *specific*

Heeft u nog **specifieke** wensen voor uw verblijf?
Do you have any **specific** wishes for your stay?

### 842 - witte [n, adj] *white*

Die **witte** tegels zijn het mooist.
Those **white** tiles are the nicest.

### 843 - hoor [v, interj] *to hear (1<sup>st</sup> and 2<sup>nd</sup> person - present tense); ~ eh, interjection used to emphatically confirm*

Je mag niet de hele pizza alleen opeten **hoor**!
You can't eat the whole pizza by yourself, **eh**!

### 844 - i [n] *the letter I*

De **i** is één van de vijf klinkers.
**The letter I** is one of the five vowels.

### 845 - buurt [n] *neighborhood; vicinity*

Er zijn geen speeltuinen in de **buurt**.
There aren't any playgrounds in the **vicinity**.

### 846 - netwerk [n, v] *network, to network (1ˢᵗ and 2ⁿᵈ person - present tense)*

Een goed professioneel **netwerk** is onbetaalbaar.
A good professional **network** is priceless.

### 847 - koffie [n] *coffee*

**Koffie** is recentelijk ongelofelijk populair geworden.
**Coffee** has recently become incredibly popular.

### 848 - overzicht [n] *overview; summary*

Dit document begint met een **overzicht** van het project.
This document starts with an **overview** of the project.

### 849 - geschreven [v] *written (past participle)*

De schrijver Harry Mulisch heeft meerdere boeken **geschreven**.
Author Harry Mulisch has **written** several books.

### 850 - niemand [pron] *nobody*

**Niemand** is perfect.

**Nobody** is perfect.

### 851 - afstand [n] *distance*

De **afstand** tussen Parijs en Berlijn is achthonderdachtenzeventig kilometer.

The **distance** between Paris and Berlin is eight hundred seventy-eight kilometers.

### 852 - ontwerp [n, v] *design; to design (1ˢᵗ and 2ⁿᵈ person - present tense)*

De student is met een ingewikkeld **ontwerp** bezig.

The student is working on an intricate **design**.

### 853 - keuken [n] *kitchen*

Dit huis heeft een ruime, moderne **keuken**.

This house has a spacious, modern **kitchen**.

### 854 - voelen [v] *to feel (infinitive and plural subjects - present tense)*

Waarom **voelen** jullie je zo moe vandaag?

Why do you **feel** so tired today?

### 855 - verschil [n, v] *difference; to be different (1ˢᵗ and 2ⁿᵈ person - present tense)*

Een klein detail maakt soms een groot **verschil**.

A small detail can sometimes make a big **difference**.

### 856 - word [v] *to become; to get + adjective (1ˢᵗ and 2ⁿᵈ person - present tense)*

Ik **word** snel ongeduldig als ik lang moet wachten.

I **get** impatient quickly when I have to wait for a long time.

**857 - uitgebreid** [adj, adv, v] *elaborate(ly); expanded (past participle)*

Het diner-buffet was ontzettend **uitgebreid**.
The dinner buffet was incredibly **elaborate**.

**858 - plezier** [n] *pleasure; fun; to please (1$^{st}$ and 2$^{nd}$ person - present tense)*

Veel **plezier** op het uitje!
Have **fun** at your excursion!

**859 - partij** [n] *(political) party; match*

De Nieuw-Vlaamse Alliantie is de grootste Vlaamse **partij**.
The Nieuw-Vlaamse Alliantie is the biggest Flemish **party**.

**860 – a.** [n] *abbreviation for "aan", meaning on, at*

Mijn familie komt uit de stad Alphen **a.**d. Rijn.
My family is from the city of Alphen **a.**d. Rijn

**861 - software** [n] *software*

De meeste **software** moet je regelmatig updaten.
You have to update most **software** regularly.

**862 - groter** [adj, adv] *bigger; taller*

Na het regenseizoen waren de planten een stuk **groter**.
After the rain season the plants were a lot **bigger**.

**863 - geef** [v] *to give (1$^{st}$ and 2$^{nd}$ person - present tense)*

**Geef** jij deze CD's aan je broer?
Will you **give** these CDs to your brother?

**864 - bevat** [v] *to contain (singular subjects - present*

*tense)*

Dit supplement **bevat** vitamine C.
This supplement **contains** vitamin C.

### 865 - vraagt [v] *to ask (2ⁿᵈ and 3ʳᵈ person - present tense)*

De verkoper **vraagt** of de klant een tas wil.
The salesman **asks** if the customer wants a bag.

### 866 - zaak [n] *business; lawsuit*

Deze **zaak** is zes maanden geleden gesloten.
This **business** closed six months ago.

### 867 - partner [n] *partner (romantic or business)*

Mag ik u aan mijn **partner** voorstellen?
May I introduce you to my **partner**?

### 868 - België [n] *Belgium*

**België** staat bekend om zijn lekkere chocolade en bier.
**Belgium** is known for its delicious chocolate and beer.

### 869 - kunst [n, adj] *art; feat; artificial*

Moderne **kunst** is vaak abstracter dan klassiekere stijlen.
Modern **art** is often more abstract than more classic styles.

### 870 - sprake [n] *talk of (mostly used in set expressions)*

Haar woedeprobleem kwam **ter sprake**.
Her anger problem **came up in conversation**.

### 871 - helpt [v] *to help (2ⁿᵈ and 3ʳᵈ person - present tense)*

Bij hoofdpijn **helpt** water drinken vaak.

Drinking water often **helps** with a headache.

### 872 - vrije [adj] *free; available; unrestricted*

De werknemers kregen als bonus een extra **vrije** dag.
The employees got an extra day **off** as a bonus.

### 873 - woensdag [n] *Wednesday*

Volgende week **woensdag** komt mijn neef uit Rusland.
Next **Wednesday,** my cousin from Russia will come.

### 874 - heer [n] *lord; sir; man; ruler*

**Heer** Janssen, dit is uw tafel.
**Sir** Janssen, this is your table.

### 875 - invloed [n] *influence*

Muziek heeft veel **invloed** over onze emoties.
Music has a lot of **influence** over our emotions.

### 876 - punt [n] *point; tip; full stop*

Team A wint daarvoor een extra **punt**.
Team A wins an extra **point** for that.

### 877 - zes [num] *six*

Een dobbelsteen heeft **zes** kanten.
A die has **six** sides.

### 878 - gezegd [v] *said (past participle)*

Je hebt niets **gezegd** over de verrassing, toch?
You haven't **said** anything about the surprise, right?

### 879 - persoonlijk [adj, adv] *in person; personal(ly)*

Hij nam die opmerking erg **persoonlijk** op.

He took that comment very **personally**.

### 880 - levert [v] *to provide; to deliver; to ship (2ⁿᵈ and 3ʳᵈ person - present tense)*

De vrachtwagen **levert** de producten vandaag om vier uur.
The truck will **deliver** the products today at four.

### 881 - c [n] *the letter C*

Mijn naam is Carien, met een **c**, niet een k.
My name is Carien, with a **C** not a K.

### 882 - dragen [v] *to carry; to wear (infinitive and plural subjects - present tense)*

De paarden **dragen** de zakken.
The horses are **carrying** the sacks.

### 883 - toepassing [n] *use; application*

De **toepassing** van de methode was moeilijker dan verwacht.
The **application** of the method was more difficult than expected.

### 884 - veilig [adj, adv] *safe, secure*

's Avonds is deze stad niet erg **veilig**.
At night this city isn't very **safe**.

### 885 - moeite [n] *difficulty; effort*

Die film is de **moeite** waard.
That movie is worth the **effort**. (*worth it*)

### 886 - merk [n, v] *mark; brand; to realize (1ˢᵗ and 2ⁿᵈ person - present tense)*

Welk **merk** tennisracket raadt u aan?
Which tennis racket **brand** do you recommend?

### 887 - past [v] *to fit; to try on (2nd and 3rd person - present tense)*

De riem **past** niet.
The belt doesn't **fit**.

### 888 - gaf [v] *to give (singular subjects - past tense)*

Waarom **gaf** zij haar hond weg?
Why did she **give** away her dog?

### 889 - reeds [adv] *already; yet*

De katten hadden **reeds** gegeten.
The cats had **already** eaten.

### 890 - reacties [n] *reactions*

Had de presentatrice zoveel **reacties** verwacht?
Had the presenter expected that many **reactions**?

### 891 - geboren [v] *born (past participle)*

Waar zijn jullie **geboren**?
Where were you **born**?

### 892 - gezet [adj, v] *plump; put, placed (past participle)*

Ik heb de borden naast de glazen **gezet**.
I've **put** the plates next to the glasses.

### 893 - veiligheid [n] *safety*

**Veiligheid** staat voorop, dus iedereen zijn riem om!
**Safety** comes first, so everyone put their seatbelts on!

### 894 - jong [n, adj] *young (animal or person); boy*

Mijn moeder was erg **jong** toen ze trouwde.

My mother was quite **young** when she got married.

### 895 - spreken [v] *to speak (infinitive and plural subjects - present tense)*

Kunnen wij de directeur **spreken**?
Can we **speak** to the director?

### 896 - gebouw [n] *building*

Er werken zevenentachtig mensen in dit **gebouw**.
Eighty-seven people work in this **building**.

### 897 - liefst [adj, adv] *sweetest; preferably; no less than*

Van alle meisjes vond Nico Madeleine het **liefst**.
Nico thought Madeleine was the **sweetest** out of all the girls.

### 898 - vertrouwen [n, v] *trust; to trust (infinitive and plural subjects - present tense)*

**Vertrouwen** jullie die advocaten honderd procent?
Do you **trust** those lawyers one hundred percent?

### 899 - passen [v] *to fit; to try on (infinitive and plural subjects - present tense)*

Je moet altijd beide schoenen **passen**, voor de zekerheid.
You must always **try on** both shoes, just in case.

### 900 - sfeer [n] *atmosphere*

Er hing een heerlijke **sfeer** op het verjaardagsfeest.
There was a lovely **atmosphere** at the birthday party.

### 901 - weekend [n] *weekend*

Zullen we dit **weekend** gaan kamperen?
Shall we go camping this **weekend**?

## 902 - bijdrage [n] *contribution; input*

Wilt u een **bijdrage** leveren aan onze campagne?
Would you like to make a **contribution** to our campaign?

## 903 - hond [n] *dog*

Ik heb drie katten, maar geen **hond**.
I have three cats but no **dog**.

## 904 - verwacht [adj, v] *expected (past participle)*

Ik had het einde van de film niet **verwacht**!
I hadn't **expected** the end of the movie!

## 905 - gedrag [n] *behaviour*

Het **gedrag** van het kind was veel verbeterd.
The child's **behaviour** had improved a lot.

## 906 - gekregen [v] *received (past participle)*

Het meisje had een bos rozen **gekregen**.
The girl had **received** a bunch of roses.

## 907 - voordeel [n] *advantage; benefit*

De atleet had een oneerlijk **voordeel**.
The athlete had an unfair **advantage**.

## 908 - kost [n, v] *cost; to cost (singular subjects - present tense)*

Hoeveel **kost** het doosje eieren?
How much does the carton of eggs **cost**?

## 909 - groepen [n] *groups; grades (at school)*

Laten we het team in twee **groepen** verdelen.

Let's divide the team into two **groups**.

### 910 - schade [n] *damage*

De orkaan had veel **schade** veroorzaakt.
The hurricane had caused a lot of **damage**.

### 911 - overigens [adv] *anyway; by the way*

Goed gedaan, **overigens**.
Well done, **by the way**.
### 912 – e-mail [n] *email*
De vrouw concentreerde zich op de belangrijke **e-mail**.
The woman was concentrating on the important **email**.

### 913 - inzicht [n] *insight; understanding*

Meditatie kan heel veel **inzicht** geven.
Meditation can bring a lot of **insight**.

### 914 - last [n, v] *load; burden; bother; pain; to weld ($2^{nd}$ and $3^{rd}$ person - present tense)*

Ze had weer **last** van haar knie.
Her knee was **bothering** her again.

### 915 - winkel [n] *store; to shop ($1^{st}$ and $2^{nd}$ person - present tense)*

Het was heel druk in de **winkel** vandaag.
It was very busy at the **store** today.

### 916 - overal [n, adv] *overall; everywhere*

Waarom ligt hier **overal** speelgoed?
Why are there toys lying around **everywhere**?

### 917 - oog [n, v] *eye; to look ($1^{st}$ and $2^{nd}$ person - present*

*tense)*

Er kwam een vlieg in zijn **oog**.
A fly got into his **eye**.

### 918 - zomer [n] *summer*

Deze **zomer** ga ik niet op vakantie.
This **summer**, I won't go on holiday.

### 919 - onderhoud [n, v] *maintenance; to maintain (1st and 2nd person - present tense)*

De auto heeft weer **onderhoud** nodig.
The car needs **maintenance** again.

### 920 - waaronder [adv] *including; such as; among which*

Zes landen hebben de EU gesticht, **waaronder** Nederland en België.
Six countries founded the EU, **including** The Netherlands and Belgium.

### 921 - overleg [n, v] *meeting; deliberation; to discuss (1st and 2nd person - present tense)*

Beide partijen gaven hun mening tijdens het **overleg**.
Both parties gave their opinion during the **meeting**.

### 922 - eventueel [adj, adv] *in case; possibly; potentially*

We kunnen **eventueel** een extra serveerster inhuren.
We can **potentially** hire an extra waitress.

### 923 - werkzaamheden [n] *(business) activities; works*

Er zijn volgende week **werkzaamheden** aan de A12.
Next week there are **works** on the A12.

### 924 - super [adj, adv, interj] *super*

De studenten waren **super** enthousiast over het project.

The students were **super** enthusiastic about the project.

### 925 - bewoners [n] *residents*

De **bewoners** van deze flat zijn goed georganiseerd.

The **residents** of this apartment building are well-organized.

### 926 - technische [adj] *technical*

Is de de **technische** dienst bij de garantie inbegrepen?

Is the **technical** service included in the warranty?

### 927 - termijn [n] *time period; deadline; installment; term*

Het bedrijf hoopt zich op korte **termijn** uit te breiden.

The company hopes to expand in the short **term**.

### 928 - gegaan [v] *gone (past participle)*

Is alles goed **gegaan** met je presentatie?

Has everything **gone** well with your presentation?

### 929 - gemeenten [n] *municipalities; districts, gathering of believers*

Noord-Holland heeft zevenenveertig **gemeenten**.

Noord-Holland has forty-seven **municipalities**.

### 930 - museum [n] *museum*

Zullen we zaterdag naar het nieuwe **museum** gaan?

Shall we go to the new **museum** on Saturday?

### 931 - d. [n] *the letter D; abbreviation for the articles "de,*

*den, der" (the)*

De naam Edwin van der Sar kan ook als Edwin v.**d.** Sar worden geschreven.
The name Edwin van der Sar can also be written Edwin v.**d.** Sar.

### 932 - ene [n, adj, art] *one; a certain*

Soms gaan instructies het **ene** oor in en gelijk het andere oor weer uit.
Sometimes instructions go in **one** ear and immediately go out the other.

### 933 - betere [adj] *better*

De serveerster was op zoek naar een **betere** baan.
The waitress was looking for a **better** job.

### 934 - maximaal [adj, adv] *maximal; a maximum of*

Ik kan **maximaal** twintig kilometer per dag lopen.
I can walk a **maximum** of twenty kilometers a day.

### 935 - plannen [n, v] *plan; to plan (plural subjects - present tense)*

Hebben jullie al **plannen** voor dit weekend?
Have you got **plans** for this weekend yet?

### 936 - vorig [adj] *former; previous, last*

**Vorig** jaar had het bedrijf meer winst gemaakt.
The company had made more profit **last** year.

### 937 - p. [n] *the letter P; common abbreviation for "per"*

De rondreis kost 350 euro **p.**p. (per persoon)
The tour costs 350 euros **p.**p. (per person)

### 938 - dinsdag [n] *Tuesday*

Op **dinsdag** zijn de bioscoopkaartjes 30% goedkoper!
On **Tuesday**, cinema tickets are 30% off!

### 939 - scholen [n, v] *schools; to school (plural subjects - present tense); to hide, to take shelter (plural subjects - past tense)*

Hoeveel **scholen** zijn er in jouw dorp?
How many **schools** are there in your village?

### 940 - regels [n] *rules; lines (in a text)*

**Regels** zijn **regels**, zonder uitzonderingen.
**Rules** are **rules**, no exceptions.

### 941 - aanpak [n] *approach*

De lerares had een hele goede **aanpak** voor moeilijke studenten.
The teacher had a very good **approach** for difficult students.

### 942 - vlak [n, adj, adv] *side; flat; plain; right, just*

Er is een speeltuin **vlak** naast ons huis.
There's a playground **right** next to our house.

### 943 - eisen [n, v] *demands, requirements; to demand (plural subjects - present tense)*

Wat zijn de belangrijkste **eisen**?
What are the main **requirements**?

### 944 - klachten [n] *complaints*

Het hotel ontving veel **klachten** over het eten.
The hotel received many **complaints** about the food.

### 945 - volledige [adj] *complete*

De **volledige** versie van het concert staat nu online.
The **complete** version of the concert is now online.

### 946 - park [n] *park*

Dit **park** is ideaal voor picknicks.
This **park** is ideal for picnics.

### 947 - voelt [v] *to feel (2<sup>nd</sup> and 3<sup>rd</sup> person - present tense)*

De president **voelt** de druk van het kabinet.
The president **feels** the pressure of the Cabinet.

### 948 - zee [n] *sea*

Het waait vaak dichtbij de **zee**.
It's often windy close to the **sea**.

### 949 - professionele [adj] *professional*

De vrouw moet **professionele** hulp inschakelen voor haar
problemen.
The woman has to get **professional** help for her problems.

### 950 - haag [n] *hedge*

We hebben de **haag** gisteren laten snoeien.
We had the **hedge** trimmed yesterday.

### 951 - cultuur [n] *culture; cultivation*

Welke **cultuur** interesseert je het meest?
Which **culture** interests you most?

### 952 - duurzame [adj] *durable; sustainable*

Veel mensen schakelen over naar **duurzame** energie.

Many people are switching to **sustainable** energy.

### 953 - verbeteren [v] *to improve; to correct (infinitive and plural subjects - present tense)*

De balletdanseres werkt hard om haar techniek te **verbeteren**.
The ballet dancer is working hard to **improve** her technique.

### 954 - toegang [n] *entrance; access*

De VIP-pasjes gaven ons **toegang** tot een speciale VIP-lounge.
The VIP passes gave us **access** to a special VIP lounge.

### 955 - club [n] *club*

Er is onlangs een nieuwe **club** voor ouderen geopend.
A new **club** for elderly people was opened recently.

### 956 - voordelen [n] *advantages, benefits*

Zelfstandig werken biedt veel **voordelen**.
Working freelance offers many **advantages**.

### 957 - organiseren [v] *to organize (infinitive and plural subjects - present tense)*

De gemeente gaat een sportwedstrijd **organiseren**.
The municipality is going to **organize** a sports match.

### 958 - voorzitter [n] *president; chairman*

De **voorzitter** kan vandaag de vergadering helaas niet bijwonen.
Unfortunately, the **chairman** can't attend today's meeting.

### 959 - laag [n, adj] *layer; low; mean*

Deze taart heeft een **laag** chocoladesaus in het midden.
This cake has a **layer** of chocolate syrup in the middle.

### 960 - spelers [n] *players; musicians*

Hoeveel **spelers** kunnen er maximaal meedoen met dit kaartspel?
What's the maximum number of **players** that can join this card game?

### 961 - effect [n] *effect; stock; spin*

Meer bewegen heeft meestal een positief **effect** op je gezondheid.
Doing more exercise usually has a positive **effect** on your health.

### 962 - hiervan [adv] *of this; about this*

Weten je ouders **hiervan**?
Do your parents know **about this**?

### 963 - trekken [n, v] *traits; to pull; to migrate (infinitive and plural subjects - present tense)*

Deze vogels **trekken** 's winters van Canada naar het zuiden.
These birds **migrate** from Canada to the south in winter.

### 964 - band [n] *tire; tape; (musical) band; relationship (two different pronunciations, depending on the meaning)*

Maartje speelt sinds zes maanden in een **band**.
Maartje has been playing in a **band** for six months.

### 965 - dood [n, adj, v] *death, dead; to kill (1$^{st}$ and 2$^{nd}$ person - present tense)*

Deze plant is **dood**.
This plant is **dead**.

### 966 - ondernemers [n] *entrepreneurs*

Veel **ondernemers** lanceren tegenwoordig digitale startups.
Many **entrepreneurs** launch digital startups nowadays.

### 967 - moderne [adj] *modern*

Hou je meer van **moderne** of ouderwetse meubels?
Do you prefer **modern** or old-fashioned furniture?

### 968 - lucht [n, v] *air; sky; smell; to air (singular subjects - present tense)*

De **lucht** is vandaag erg grijs.
The **sky** is very gray today.

### 969 - la [n] *drawer; musical note la*

Alle schone sokken liggen in de bovenste **la**.
All the clean socks are in the top **drawer**.

### 970 - uitvoering [n] *execution; show; version*

Mijn dochters **uitvoering** is op zaterdag.
My daughter's **show** is on Saturday.

### 971 - merken [n, v] *brands; to notice; to label*

Chinese **merken** worden steeds populairder.
Chinese **brands** are getting more and more popular.

### 972 - telefoon [n] *telephone*

Kan jij de **telefoon** opnemen?
Can you answer the **telephone**?

### 973 - fijn [adj, adv] *fine(ly); nice*

Het was heel **fijn** om jullie weer te zien!
It was really **nice** to see you again!

### 974 - video [n] *video*

Er is een nieuwe **video** van je favoriete Youtuber!

There's a new **video** by your favorite Youtuber!

### 975 - mogelijke [adj] *possible; potential*

Hij had niets gehoord over een **mogelijke** treinstaking.
He hadn't heard anything about a **potential** train strike.

### 976 - digitale [adj] *digital*

**Digitale** media hebben steeds meer invloed op de samenleving.
**Digital** media have more and more of an influence on society.

### 977 - management [n] *management*

Wat heeft het **management** gezegd over je innovatieve voorstel?
What did **management** say about your innovative proposal?

### 978 - taal [n] *language*

Een buitenlandse **taal** kunnen spreken heeft veel voordelen.
Being able to speak a foreign **language** has a lot of advantages.

### 979 - ervaringen [n] *experiences*

Het meisje had veel **ervaringen** opgedaan tijdens haar reis.
The girl had gained many **experiences** during her journey.

### 980 - gehele [adj] *entire, whole*

Het slachtoffer had brandwonden over zijn **gehele** lichaam.
The victim had burns on his **entire** body.

### 981 - bouw [n, v] *construction (industry); cultivation; to build (1st and 2nd person - present tense)*

Mijn mans neef werkt in de **bouw**.
My husband's cousin works in **construction**.

### 982 - inderdaad [adv] *indeed*

Er zijn **inderdaad** nieuwe mensen in het huis hiernaast komen wonen.

New people have **indeed** moved in next door.

### 983 - politie [n] *police; police officer*

Snel, bel de **politie**!

Quick, call the **police**!

### 984 - bepalen [v] *to determine (infinitive and plural subjects - present tense)*

De leerlingen **bepalen** niet welk cijfer ze krijgen!

The pupils don't **determine** what grade they get!

### 985 - loop [n, v] *barrel; walk; course; to walk (1ˢᵗ and 2ⁿᵈ person - present tense)*

**Loop** hier rechtdoor tot het eind van de straat.

**Walk** straight until the end of the street.

### 986 - enorm [adj, adv] *enormous(ly)*

U heeft ons **enorm** geholpen.

You've helped us **enormously**.

### 987 - workshop [n] *workshop*

Die dans**workshop** interesseert me heel erg, maar is helaas te duur.

That dance **workshop** interests me a lot, but unfortunately it's too expensive.

### 988 - tegenwoordig [adv] *nowadays; currently*

Waar wonen jullie **tegenwoordig**?

Where are you living **nowadays**?

**989 - orde** [n] *order*

De leraar kon geen **orde** houden.
The teacher couldn't keep **order**.

**990 - minister** [n] *minister; secretary*

De **minister** van Defensie moest een moeilijke beslissing nemen.
The **Secretary** of Defense had to make a tough decision.

**991 - gebeuren** [n, v] *occurrence; to happen (infinitive and plural subjects - present tense)*

Zulke dingen **gebeuren** nou eenmaal.
Those things just **happen** sometimes.

**992 - hoeveel** [num] *how much/many*

**Hoeveel** slaapkamers heeft de flat?
**How many** bedrooms does the apartment have?

**993 - gewerkt** [v] *worked; functioned (past participle)*

Heb je weleens in het buitenland **gewerkt**?
Have you ever **worked** abroad?

**994 - stappen** [n, v] *steps; to go out (dancing); to step (infinitive and plural subjects - present tense)*

De baby heeft net haar eerste **stappen** genomen!
The baby has just taken her first **steps**!

**995 - baan** [n] *lane; course; job; track*

Leo kan geen **baan** vinden in zijn sector.
Leo can't find a **job** in his sector.

**996 - momenteel** [adj, adv] *at the moment, currently*

Er zijn **momenteel** geen vacatures.
There aren't any job vacancies **at the moment**.

**997 - bedoeld** [adj, adv, v] *intended; meant (past participle)*

Het was als een grapje **bedoeld**.
It was **meant** to be a joke.

**998 - versie** [n] *version; account*

Dit is niet de gecorrigeerde **versie** van haar boek, toch?
This isn't the corrected **version** of her book, is it?

**999 - vroeger** [adj, adv] *earlier; in the past*

**Vroeger** waren er minder auto's op de wegen.
**In the past** there were fewer cars on the roads.

**1000 - zoon** [n] *son*

Hoe oud is hun **zoon**?
How old is their **son**?

**1001 - zo'n** [n, adv] *such a; approximately*

Mijn dochter heeft **zo'n** mooie tekening gemaakt!
My daughter has made **such a** pretty drawing!

**1002 - miljard** [num] *billion*

Er zijn al meer dan zeven **miljard** mensen op aarde.
There are already over seven **billion** people on Earth.

**1003 - aandelen** [n] *shares*

**Aandelen** worden verkocht op de aandelenbeurs.

**Shares** are sold at the stock exchange.

### 1004 - regering [n] *government*

We zijn het niet eens met de plannen van de **regering**.
We don't agree with the plans of the **government**.

### 1005 - aandeel [n] *share*

Enkele grote bedrijven beheersen een groot **aandeel** van de markt.
A few large companies dominate a large **share** of the market.

### 1006 - politieke [adj] *political*

Wat vindt u van de **politieke** partij GroenLinks?
What do you think about the **political** party, GroenLinks?

### 1007 - omzet [n, v] *turnover, revenue*

De economische crisis heeft onze **omzet** gehalveerd!
The economic crisis has halved our **revenue**!

### 1008 - beurs [n] *wallet; scholarship; fair; stock exchange*

Op de **beurs** kan je zowel veel geld verdienen als verliezen.
At the **exchange,** you can earn or lose a lot of money.

### 1009 - winst [n] *profit*

Een hoge omzet betekent niet altijd een grote **winst**.
High revenue doesn't always equate a large **profit**.

### 1010 - economische [adj] *economic*

Hoe was de **economische** groei van Duitsland vorig jaar?
How was Germany's **economic** growth last year?

## 1011 - koers [n] *(exchange) rate; value; course*

De **koers** van aandelen stijgt of daalt soms heel plotseling.

The **value** of shares sometimes rises or falls very suddenly.

## 1012 - politiek [n, adj] *politics; policy; political*

Weet jij veel van **politiek** af?

Do you know a lot about **politics**?

## 1013 - groei [n, v] *growth; development; to grow (1$^{st}$ and 2$^{nd}$ person - present tense)*

Persoonlijke **groei** is net zo belangrijk als je carrière.

Personal **growth** is just as important as your career.

## 1014 - gulden [n, adj] *guilder (currency of The Netherlands before the euro), golden*

De Nederlandse **gulden** is op 1 januari 2002 vervangen door de euro.

The Dutch **guilder** was replaced by the Euro on January first, 2002.

## 1015 - trouwens [adv] *by the way; moreover*

**Trouwens**, hebben jullie Alfred dit weekend gezien?

**By the way**, have you seen Alfred this weekend?

## 1016 - president [n] *president; chairman*

Wie is de huidige **president** van Brazilië?

Who's the current **president** of Brazil?

## 1017 - tegenover [prep] *opposite*

Er zit een bakkerij **tegenover** de slager.

There's a bakery **opposite** the butcher's.

## 1018 - aldus [adv] *according to; thus*

De inbrekers zijn door het raam geklommen, **aldus** de politie.
The burglars climbed in through the window, **according to** the police.

## 1019 - tel [n, v] *count; second; to count (1ˢᵗ and 2ⁿᵈ person - present tense)*

**Tel** jij de borden?
Will you **count** the plates?

## 1020 - economie [n] *economy*

Zal de Belgische **economie** volgend jaar veel groeien?
Will the Belgian **economy** grow a lot next year?

## 1021 - werknemers [n] *employees*

De **werknemers** zijn niet tevreden over hun arbeidsvoorwaarden.
The **employees** aren't satisfied with their working conditions.

## 1022 - sector [n] *sector; segment*

Welke economische **sector** groeit het snelst?
Which economic **sector** is growing fastest?

## 1023 - voorbije [adj] *finished; past*

We hebben dit al besproken in de **voorbije** vergaderingen.
We've already discussed this in **past** meetings.

## 1024 - verkopen [n, v] *sales; to sell (infinitive and plural subjects - present tense)*

De man wil zijn auto **verkopen**.
The man wants to **sell** his car.

### 1025 - buitenlandse [adj] *foreign*

Mijn buurman spaart **buitenlandse** munten.
My neighbor collects **foreign** coins.

### 1026 - ondernemingen [n] *enterprises; businesses*

Steeds meer **ondernemingen** verkopen voornamelijk online.
More and more **enterprises** primarily sell online.

### 1027 - nauwelijks [adv] *hardly*

Ik had je **nauwelijks** herkend met die baard!
I **hardly** recognized you with that beard!

### 1028 - productie [n] *production*

Is de **productie** verminderd na de recessie?
Has **production** decreased after the recession?

### 1029 - onderneming [n] *enterprise; business*

Een nieuwe **onderneming** beginnen vergt veel tijd en energie.
Starting a new **business** takes a lot of time and energy.

### 1030 - verkoop [n, v] *sale; to sell (1ˢᵗ and 2ⁿᵈ person - present tense)*

Dit huis staat in de **verkoop**.
This house is for **sale**.

### 1031 - jongste [adj] *youngest*

Christine is de **jongste** van 3 zussen.
Christine is the **youngest** of three sisters.

### 1032 - des [art] *archaic way of saying "of the", mostly*

De vrouw **des** huizes.
The woman **of the** house.

### 1033 - banken [n] *banks*

Er zitten hier twee **banken** naast elkaar.
There are two **banks** next to each other here.

### 1034 - liet [v] *to let, to allow (singular subjects – past tense)*

De vader **liet** zijn dochter niet alleen naar het feestje gaan.
The father didn't **let** his daughter go to the party alone.

### 1035 - verleden [n, adj] *past*

In het **verleden** kampten minder mensen met obesitas.
In the **past**, less people struggled with obesity.

### 1036 - verkocht [v] *sold (past participle)*

De boer heeft al zijn aardappelen **verkocht**.
The farmer has **sold** all of his potatoes.

### 1037 - oorlog [n] *war*

Mijn oudoom was een belangrijke generaal in de **oorlog** in Vietnam.
My great-uncle was an important general in the **war** in Vietnam.

### 1038 - sterke [adj] *strong; potent; unbelievable*

Acrobaten hebben hele **sterke** buikspieren.
Acrobats have very **strong** abdominal muscles.

### 1039 - beleid [n] *policy*

Het nieuwe **beleid** van de burgemeester was niet erg populair.
The mayor's new **policy** wasn't very popular.

### 1041 - cijfers [n] *numbers; grades*

Sarah heeft altijd de hoogste **cijfers** in onze klas.
Sarah always gets the highest **grades** in our class.

### 1042 - info [n] *info*

We zullen je wat meer **info** per e-mail sturen.
We will send you some more **info** via email.

### 1043 - directeur [n] *director*

Mijn collega kan totaal niet overweg met onze **directeur**.
My colleague doesn't get on with our **director** at all.

### 1044 - bevolking [n] *population*

Hoe groot is de totale **bevolking** van Noorwegen?
What is the total **population** of Norway?

### 1045 - acht [num] *eight*

Een achthoek heeft **acht** zijden.
An octagon has **eight** sides.

### 1046 - zeven [num] *seven*

Waar zijn die **zeven** dwergen?
Where are those **seven** dwarves?

### 1047 - beperkt [adj, v] *limited (past participle)*

Onze kennis over computers is **beperkt**.
Our computer knowledge is **limited**.

### 1048 - zware [adj] *heavy; tough*

De wandelaars hebben allemaal een **zware** rugzak.
The hikers all have a **heavy** backpack.

### 1049 - macht [n] *power, force; authority*

Dictators snakken naar **macht**.
Dictators yearn for **power**.

### 1050 - dergelijke [adj] *such*

Ons bedrijf tolereert **dergelijke** opmerkingen niet!
Our company doesn't tolerate **such** comments!

### 1051 - klassieke [adj] *classical*

**Klassieke** muziek helpt hem te ontspannen.
**Classical** music helps him relax.

### 1052 - twintig [num] *twenty*

Er zijn **twintig** medewerkers op mijn afdeling.
There are **twenty** employees in my department.

### 1053 - premier [n] *Prime Minister*

Jan Peter Balkenende was van 2002 tot 2010 **premier** van
Nederland.
Jan Peter Balkenende was **Prime Minister** of The Netherlands
from 2002 to 2010.

### 1054 - gemiddelde [adj, adv] *(on) average*

De **gemiddelde** lengte van Nederlandse vrouwen is
honderdzevenenzestig cm.
The **average** height of Dutch women is hundred-sixty-seven cm.

**1055 - parlement** [n] *parliament*

Het Belgische **Parlement** telt in totaal tweehonderdtien zetels.
The Belgian **Parliament** has a total of two-hundred-ten seats.

**1056 - z'n** [n] *abbreviation for "zijn", meaning of "his"*

De acteur was weer **z'n** tekst kwijt!
The actor had forgotten **his** lines again!

**1057 - rente** [n] *interest*

Wat is de totale **rente** over deze lening?
What's the total **interest** on this loan?

**1059 - bedraagt** [v] *to amount to (2ⁿᵈ and 3ʳᵈ person - present tense)*

De afstand van Brussel naar Parijs **bedraagt**
tweehonderdvijfenzestig km.
The distance from Brussels to Paris **amounts to** two-hundred-sixty-five km.

**1060 - duur** [n, adj] *duration; expensive*

In Nederland is yoghurt niet **duur**.
In The Netherlands, yogurt isn't **expensive**.

**1061 - bleef** [v] *to stay; to continue (singular subjects - past tense)*

Mijn zus **bleef** deze week bij mij thuis.
My sister **stayed** at my house this week.

**1062 - denkt** [v] *to think (2ⁿᵈ and 3ʳᵈ person - present tense)*

De leerling **denkt** lang na.
The student **is thinking** for a long time.

154

**1063 - leger** [n, adj, v] *army, emptier; to encamp (1<sup>st</sup> and 2<sup>nd</sup> person - present tense)*

Mathias wilde bij het **leger**.
Mathias wanted to join the **army**.

**1064 - reeks** [n] *series; sequence*

U heeft een **reeks** boeken over honden te koop, toch?
You've got a **series** of books about dogs for sale, right?

**1065 - nam** [v] *to take (singular subjects - past tense)*

Het kindje **nam** nog een koekje.
The child **took** another cookie.

**1066 - steun** [n, v] *support; to lean on, to support (1<sup>st</sup> and 2<sup>nd</sup> person - present tense)*

Emotionele **steun** van vrienden is goud waard.
Emotional **support** from friends is golden.

**1067 - zware** [adj] *heavy; tough*

De leraren hadden een **zware** dag gehad.
The teachers had had a **tough** day.

**1068 - erop** [adv] *on it/them*

Ik heb de aardbeien **erop** gelegd.
I've put the strawberries **on it**.

**1069 - gewoon** [adj, adv] *normal; simply; as usual*

De leerling had **gewoon** geen zin om op te letten.
The student **simply** didn't feel like paying attention.

**1070 - moesten** [v] *to have to (plural subjects - past*

*tense)*

In de Middeleeuwen **moesten** de mensen veel meer lopen.
In the Middle Ages, people **had to** walk much more.

### 1071 - buitenland [n] *foreign country, abroad*

Tegenwoordig studeren meer Nederlanders in het **buitenland**.
Nowadays, more Dutch people study **abroad**.

### 1072 - stijging [n] *rise; increase*

Vorig jaar was er een verrassende **stijging** in de huizenprijzen.
Last year there was a surprising **rise** in house prices.

### 1073 - totale [adj, adv] *total(ly); entire(ly)*

De **totale** schade aan de auto bedroeg vijfhonderd euro.
The **total** damage to the car amounted to five-hundred euros.

### 1074 - nationale [adj] *national*

Hoeveel **nationale** feestdagen heeft Ierland?
Hoe many **national** holidays does Ireland have?

### 1075 - middelen [n] *waists; medication; means*

Zwangere vrouwen wordt afgeraden deze **middelen** te gebruiken.
Pregnant women are advised against using this **medication**.

### 1076 - namen [n, v] *names; to take (plural subjects - past tense)*

Gijs en Saartje zijn typisch Nederlandse **namen**.
Gijs and Saartje are typically Dutch **names**.

### 1077 - nogal [adv] *quite, rather*

Een halve kilo friet is **nogal** veel voor een person.

Half a kilo of French fries is **quite** a lot for one person.

### 1078 - hogere [adj] *higher*

De toeristen hadden **hogere** verwachtingen van het buffet.
The tourists had **higher** expectations of the buffet.

### 1079 - slecht [adj, adv] *bad*

Waarom is de wolf meestal **slecht** in kinderverhalen?
Why is the wolf usually **bad** in children's stories?

### 1080 - beroep [n, v] *profession; appeal; to appeal (1st and 2nd person - present tense)*

Wat is het **beroep** van uw echtgenoot?
What is your spouse's **profession**?

### 1081 - zowat [adv] *almost; just about*

De serveerster had **zowat** veertien uur gewerkt zonder te stoppen!
The waitress had **almost** worked for fourteen hours non-stop!

### 1082 - grotere [adj] *bigger*

De artiest maakte steeds **grotere** standbeelden.
The artist made increasingly **bigger** statues.

### 1083 - Europees [n, adj] *European*

Welk **Europees** land ontvangt de meeste toeristen?
Which **European** country receives the most tourists?

### 1084 - kregen [v] *to receive, to get; to obtain (plural subjects - past tense)*

We **kregen** een slap antwoord op onze klacht.
We **received** a poor reply to our complaint.

### 1085 - minstens [adv] *at least*

Het opstel moet **minstens** duizend woorden tellen.
The essay has to be **at least** a thousand words long.

### 1086 - beleggers [n] *investors*

**Beleggers** lezen veel over de aandelenbeurzen.
**Investors** read a lot about the stock exchanges.

### 1087 - centrale [adj] *central; main*

Het **centrale** idee van de toespraak was niet duidelijk.
The **main** idea of the speech wasn't clear.

### 1088 - gevolgen [n] *consequences*

Langdurig drugsmisbruik heeft ernstige **gevolgen**.
Long-term drug abuse has serious **consequences**.

### 1089 - l [n] *the letter L*

Kan jij tien groentes noemen die met een l beginnen?
Can you name ten vegetables that start with the letter **L**?

### 1090 - strijd [n, v] *struggle; conflict; combat; to struggle, to fight (1st and 2nd person - present tense)*

We moeten de **strijd** tegen armoede niet opgeven!
We mustn't give up the **fight** against poverty!

### 1091 - akkoord [n] *agreement*

De partijen konden geen **akkoord** bereiken.
The parties couldn't reach an **agreement**.

### 1092 - gang [n] *course; hallway*

De kapstok staat in de **gang**.

The coat rack is in the **hallway**.

### 1093 - voorlopig [adj, adv] *for now; temporary; temporarily*

Ik heb **voorlopig** geen plannen om te verhuizen.
I don't have any plans to move **for now**.

### 1094 - praten [v] *to talk (infinitive and plural subjects - present tense)*

De baas wilde met zijn team **praten**.
The boss wanted to **talk** to his team.

### 1095 - kader [n] *textbox; framework; management; as part of*

Vrijdag is het grote feest in het **kader** van ons jubileum.
Friday is the big party **as part of** our anniversary.

### 1096 - telkens [adv] *every time; repeatedly; more and more*

Waarom vergeet je **telkens** weer je sleutels?
Why do you **repeatedly** forget your keys?

### 1097 - concurrentie [n] *competition*

De **concurrentie** onder professionele dansers is hevig.
**Competition** among professional dancers is fierce.

### 1098 - verband [n] *bandage; connection; cooperation*

Er was een **verband** tussen de twee aanvallen.
There was a **connection** between the two attacks.

### 1099 - kapitaal [n, adj] *capital; enormous*

Heeft hij genoeg **kapitaal** om de onderneming te starten?

Does he have enough **capital** to start the business?

### 1100 - gemiddeld [adj, adv] *(on) average*

Hoeveel verdient een metselaar **gemiddeld**?
How much does a bricklayer earn **on average**?

### 1101 - rendement [n] *profit; yield*

De meeste beleggers berekenen ieder jaar het **rendement** van hun investeringen.
Most investors calculate the **profit** of their investments every year.

### 1102 - personeel [n] *personnel*

De afdeling personeelszaken neemt het nieuwe **personeel** aan.
The human resources department hires new **personnel**.

### 1103 - schreef [v] *to write (singular subjects - past tense)*

Jij **schreef** hele mooie gedichten op school!
You **wrote** very nice poems at school!

### 1104 - tafel [n] *table*

De **tafel** staat in een hoek, met vier stoelen eromheen.
The **table** is in a corner with four chairs around it.

### 1105 - gisteren [adv] *yesterday*

Er was **gisteren** een tsunami in Japan!
There was a tsunami in Japan **yesterday**!

### 1106 - verwachten [v] *to expect (infinitive and plural subjects - present tense)*

Je ouders **verwachten** dat je goede cijfers haalt.
Your parents **expect** you to get good grades.

160

### 1107 - zwarte [n, adj] *black*

Door **zwarte** kleding lijk je vaak slanker.
**Black** clothes tend to make you look slimmer.

### 1108 - j [n] *the letter J*

In de klas zitten vijf meisjes wier naam met een **j** begint.
In the class, there are five girls whose name starts with a **J**.

### 1109 - controle [n] *control; inspection*

De man verloor de **controle** over het stuur.
The man lost **control** of the steering wheel.

### 1110 - verlies [n, v] *loss; to lose (1$^{st}$ and 2$^{nd}$ person - present tense)*

Ik **verlies** weddenschappen bijna altijd!
I almost always **lose** bets!

### 1111 - enorme [adj] *enormous*

Er zijn **enorme** insecten in het regenwoud.
There are **enormous** insects in the rainforest.

### 1112 - studie [n] *course; research*

Hoe lang duurt je **studie**?
How long does your **course** last?

### 1113 - onlangs [adv] *recently*

Onze familie is **onlangs** gaan zeilen op het IJsselmeer.
Our family **recently** went sailing on Lake IJssel.

### 1114 - stukken [n] *pieces; works; items; documents*

Deze puzzel heeft duizend **stukken**.
This jigsaw has a thousand **pieces**.

## 1115 - verkiezingen [n] *elections*

De meeste **verkiezingen** zijn iedere vier jaar.
The majority of **elections** happen every four years.

## 1116 - wijn [n] *wine*

De Russische man hield niet van **wijn**.
The Russian man didn't like **wine**.

## 1117 - lage [adj] *low; mean*

Wat denk je dat die **lage,** donkere wolken betekenen?
What do you think those **low**, dark clouds mean?

## 1118 - les [n] *lesson, class; to take driver's lessons (1ˢᵗ and 2ⁿᵈ person - present tense)*

Morgen hebben we een hele interessante **les**!
Tomorrow we'll have a very interesting **lesson**!

## 1119 - eveneens [conj] *also, too*

De winkel verkoopt behalve tuingereedschap **eveneens** planten.
The store, apart from garden equipment, **also** sells plants.

## 1120 - zogenaamde [adj] *so-called, supposed*

De **zogenaamde** waarzegster voorspelde mijn toekomst.
The **so-called** fortune teller predicted my future.

## 1121 - legt [v] *to lay; to put (2ⁿᵈ and 3ʳᵈ person - present tense)*

De winkelbediende **legt** het wisselgeld op de toonbank.
The shop assistant **puts** the change on the counter.

## 1122 - wellicht [adj] *perhaps, maybe*

**Wellicht** hebben jullie morgenochtend tijd voor de vergadering?

**Perhaps** you'll have time for the meeting tomorrow morning?

### 1123 - dertig [num] *thirty*

Veertig is het nieuwe **dertig**, toch?
Forty is the new **thirty**, right?

### 1124 - noemen [v] *to call; to mention; to name (infinitive and plural subjects - present tense)*

Hoe **noemen** ze deze bloem in jouw regio?
What do they **call** this flower in your region?

### 1125 - lager [adj, adv] *lower; meaner*

Nederland ligt veel **lager** dan Zwitserland.
The Netherlands lies much **lower** than Switzerland.

### 1126 - hoofdstad [n] *capital*

Wat is de **hoofdstad** van Nederland, Den Haag of Amsterdam?
What's the **capital** of The Netherlands, The Hague or Amsterdam?

### 1127 - verloren [adj, v] *lost (past participle)*

Het Duitse hockeyteam had van het Poolse team **verloren**.
The German hockey team had **lost** against the Polish team.

### 1128 - crisis [n] *crisis*

In 2008 was er een ernstige economische **crisis**.
In 2008, there was a serious economic **crisis**.

### 1129 - heet [adj, v] *hot; spicy; to be called (singular subjects - present tense)*

Hoe **heet** deze straat?
What's this street **called**?

**1130 - ton** [n, adj] *barrel; (metric) ton; 100,000 (km, money)*

Dit huis is een **ton** meer waard dan vijftien jaar geleden!
This house is worth a **hundred thousand** more than fifteen years ago!

**1131 - leidt** [v] *to lead (to) (2<sup>nd</sup> and 3<sup>rd</sup> person - present tense)*

De boeddhistische monnik **leidt** een kalm, meditatief leven.
The Buddhist monk **leads** a calm, meditative life.

**1132 - kilometer** [n] *kilometer*

Over een **kilometer** moeten we links afslaan.
In one **kilometer** we have to take the left exit.

**1133 - ogenblik** [n] *moment*

Een **ogenblik** alstublieft, ik ben zo bij u.
One **moment** please, I'll be with you in a moment.

**1134 - volgend** [adj, v] *next; to follow (present participle)*

De studenten gaan **volgend** weekend op studiereis.
The students are going on a study trip **next** weekend.

**1135 - portefeuille** [n] *wallet; portfolio*

Meneer, is dit uw **portefeuille**?
Sir, is this your **wallet**?

**1136 - één** [num] *one (emphasizing the number)*

Er is nog maar **één** wc-rol over.
There's only **one** toilet roll left.

### 1137 - veranderingen [n] *changes*

Onze oma heeft veel **veranderingen** doorgemaakt.
Our grandma has experienced many **changes**.

### 1138 - investeringen [n] *investments*

In tijden van crisis verminderen de nieuwe **investeringen** meestal.
In times of crisis, new **investments** usually decrease.

### 1139 - maatregelen [n] *measures*

Het bestuur besloot drastische **maatregelen** te nemen in verband met de crisis.
Management decided to take drastic **measures** due to the crisis.

### 1140 - honderd [num] *one hundred*

Vijftig plus vijftig is **honderd**.
Fifty plus fifty is **one hundred**.

### 1141 - tentoonstelling [n] *exhibition*

Zou je mee willen naar de Karel Appel **tentoonstelling** op zaterdag?
Would you like to come along to the Karel Appel **exhibition** on Saturday?

### 1142 - smaak [n, v] *taste; flavor; to taste (passive verb, 1st and 2nd person - present tense)*

Indisch eten heeft een pittige **smaak**.
Indian food has a spicy **flavor**.

### 1143 - recente [adj] *recent*

De **recente** gebeurtenissen in het Midden-Oosten zijn zorgwekkend.

The **recent** events in the Middle East are worrying.

### 1144 - bracht [v] *to bring (singular subjects - past tense)*

Mijn man **bracht** me heerlijke truffels voor mijn verjaardag!
My husband **brought** me delicious truffles for my birthday!

### 1145 - tegelijk [adv] *at the same time*

Kinderen, niet allemaal **tegelijk** praten!
Kids, don't all talk **at the same time**!

### 1146 - steeg [n, v] *alley; to rise (singular subjects - past tense)*

Er wonen vast ratten in die **steeg**.
Surely, rats live in that **alley**.

### 1147 - traditionele [adj] *traditional*

**Traditionele** Nederlandse klederdracht is heel kleurrijk.
**Traditional** Dutch folkloric costume is very colorful.

### 1148 - evolutie [n] *evolution*

De **evolutie** van dieren bestuderen is hartstikke interessant.
Studying animal **evolution** is incredibly interesting.

### 1149 - stijl [n, adj] *style; stile, steep*

"De **Stijl**" was een Nederlandse kunstbeweging opgezet in 1917.
"The **Style**" was a Dutch art movement founded in 1917.

### 1150 - amper [adv] *barely*

Ik kon mijn Nederlandse lerares **amper** begrijpen.
I could **barely** understand my Dutch teacher.

### 1151 - contract [n] *contract*

Beide partijen hebben het **contract** ondertekend.
Both parties have signed the **contract**.

### 1152 - lijn [n, v] *(telephone) line; plot; to diet (1ˢᵗ and 2ⁿᵈ person - present tense)*

Toon, je moeder is aan de **lijn**!
Toon, your mum is on the **line**!

### 1153 - bezit [n, v] *property; to own (singular subjects - present tense)*

De miljonair **bezit** vijf villa's in Zuid-Frankrijk.
The millionaire **owns** five villas in the south of France.

### 1154 - betaalt [v] *to pay (2ⁿᵈ and 3ʳᵈ person - present tense)*

Tanja's nieuw baan **betaalt** heel goed.
Tanja's new job **pays** very well.

### 1155 - beelden [n] *statues; images; stills*

De cameraman had mooie **beelden** vastgelegd.
The cameraman captured beautiful **images**.

### 1156 - meerderheid [n] *majority*

De **meerderheid** beslist.
The **majority** decides.

### 1157 - haalt [v] *to bring; to get; to manage; to achieve something (2ⁿᵈ and 3ʳᵈ person - present tense)*

Op zondag **haalt** mijn broer altijd ijs als toetje.
On Sundays, my brother always **gets** icecream for dessert.

**1158 - telt** [v] *to count (2nd and 3rd person - present tense)*

De **caissière** telt de biljetten.
The **cashier** counts the bills.

**1159 - vertelt** [v] *to tell (2nd and 3rd person - present tense); miscounted (past participle)*

Mijn opa **vertelt** altijd hele gekke verhalen.
My grandfather always **tells** really crazy stories.

**1160 - liever** [adj, adv] *sweeter; preferably, rather*

Karel drinkt **liever** thee dan koffie.
Karel would **rather** drink tea than coffee.

**1161 - erin** [adv] *in it/them*

Daar is de tas, doe je deze sokken **erin**?
The bag is over there, will you put these socks **in it**?

**1162 - morgen** [n, adv] *morning; tomorrow*

De advocaat heeft **morgen** een belangrijke hoorzitting.
The lawyer has an important hearing **tomorrow**.

**1163 - toont** [v] *to show (2nd and 3rd person - present tense)*

De reiziger **toont** zijn kaartje aan de conducteur.
The traveler **shows** his ticket to the inspector.

**1164 - positie** [n] *position; situation; job*

Wat is de huidige **positie** van het vliegtuig?
What is the current **position** of the airplane?

**1165 - positief** [adj, adv] *positive*

Onze lerares is bijna altijd heel **positief**.
Our teacher is nearly always very **positive**.

**1166 - lijken** [n, v] *corpses; to seem; to look alike
(infinitive and plural subjects - present tense)*

Mijn nieuwe collega's **lijken** heel aardig te zijn.
My new coworkers **seem** to be very nice.

**1167 - jaarlijks** [adj, adv] *yearly*

Krijg jij **jaarlijks** loonsverhoging?
Do you get a raise **yearly**?

**1168 - bedoeling** [n] *purpose, intention*

Sorry, het was niet de **bedoeling** zo laat te komen.
Sorry, it wasn't our **intention** to get here this late.

**1169 - foto's** [n] *photos*

Janine had mooie **foto's** gemaakt van haar familie.
Janine had taken beautiful **photos** of her family.

**1170 - beslissing** [n] *decision*

Weet je zeker dat het de juiste **beslissing** is?
Are you sure it's the right **decision**?

**1171 - kabinet** [n] *display case; cabinet*

Het Nederlandse **kabinet** bestaat uit ministers en
staatssecretarissen.
The Dutch **cabinet** consists of ministers and state secretaries.

**1172 - betaald** [v] *paid (past participle)*

Jouw zus heeft de rekening **betaald**.

Your sister has **paid** the bill.

### 1173 - wagen [n, v] *cart; vehicle; to dare (infinitive and plural subjects - present tense)*

Petra doet de boodschappen in de **wagen**.
Petra puts the groceries in the **cart**.

### 1174 - belangstelling [n] *interest*

Wij hebben veel **belangstelling** voor de Griekse oudheid.
We have a lot of **interest** in Ancient Greece.

### 1175 - voorstel [n] *proposal*

Onze boekhouder deed ons een aantrekkelijk zakelijk **voorstel**.
Our bookkeeper made us an attractive business **proposal**.

### 1176 - noemt [v] *to call; to mention; to name (2nd and 3rd person - present tense)*

De student **noemt** alle hoofdsteden van Europa.
The student **names** all the European capitals.

### 1177 - vermogen [n] *power; capacity; capital, assets*

Door investeringen had de belegger een flink **vermogen** opgebouwd.
Through investments, the investor had acquired a sizable **capital**.

### 1178 - indruk [n] *impression*

De sollicitant wilde een goede eerste **indruk** maken op de interviewer.
The job applicant wanted to leave a good first **impression** with the interviewer.

### 1179 - markten [n] *markets*

Welke **markten** raadt u me aan in Antwerpen?
Which **markets** in Antwerp can you recommend?

### 1180 - model [n] *model; version*

Famke Janssen begon als **model** en werd daarna actrice.
Famke Janssen started as a **model** and then became an actress.

### 1181 - dochter [n] *daughter*

Onze **dochter** is cardioloog.
Our **daughter** is a cardiologist.

### 1182 - hangt [v] *to hang (on the wall) (2$^{nd}$ and 3$^{rd}$ person - present tense)*

Je zomerjas **hangt** in de kast.
Your summer coat **is hanging** in the closet.

### 1183 - kwestie [n] *issue; dispute; question*

Helen is een **kwestie** van tijd.
Healing is a **matter** of time.

### 1184 - steden [n] *cities*

Sommige mensen houden niet van grote **steden**.
Some people don't like big **cities**.

### 1185 - gebrek [n] *lack; handicap; defect*

In ontwikkelingslanden is er vaak een **gebrek** aan schoon
drinkwater.
In developing countries, there's often a **lack** of clean drinking
water.

**1186 - commissie** [n] *commission; committee*

Verdient dat uitzendbureau veel **commissie**?
Does that employment agency earn a lot of **commission**?

**1187 - verliezen** [n, v] *losses; to lose (infinitive and plural subjects - present tense)*

De peuter kon niet tegen **verliezen**.
The toddler couldn't handle **losing**.

**1188 - vormt** [v] *to mold; to constitute; to shape (2nd and 3rd person - present tense)*

Het kind **vormt** een hondje met klei.
The child **molds** a dog out of clay.

**1189 - gesloten** [adj, v] *closed (past participle)*

De bakkerij is op zondag **gesloten**.
The bakery is **closed** on Sundays.

**1190 - viel** [v] *to fall (singular subjects - past tense)*

De bal **viel** uit haar handen.
The ball **fell** from her hands.

**1191 - ministerie** [n] *ministry*

Zijn vrouw werkt bij het **Ministerie** van Financiën.
His wife works at the **Ministry** of Finance.

**1192 - titel** [n] *title*

Ik herinner me de **titel** van dat mooie boek niet.
I don't remember the **title** of that beautiful book.

**1193 - voortdurend** [adj, adv] *permanent(ly);*

172

*constant(ly)*

Mijn opa rookte **voortdurend** sigaretten.
My grandfather used to **constantly** smoke cigarettes.

### 1194 - volle [adj] *full; entire*

Sporten met een **volle** maag is ongezond.
Playing sports on a **full** stomach is unhealthy.

### 1195 - vergelijking [n] *comparison*

Hij is lang in **vergelijking** met zijn moeder.
He is tall in **comparison** to his mother.

### 1196 - gevraagd [adj, v] *requested; asked (past participle)*

Hij heeft me ten huwelijk **gevraagd**!
He has **asked** me to marry him!

### 1197 - onmiddellijk [adv] *immediately*

Stop **onmiddellijk** met schoppen!
Stop kicking **immediately**!

### 1198 - bereid [adj, v] *prepared, willing; to prepare (1st and 2nd person - present tense)*

De ondernemer was **bereid** om heel hard te werken.
The entrepreneur was **willing** to work very hard.

### 1199 - vijftig [num] *fifty*

Deze rugzak kost **vijftig** euro.
This backpack costs **fifty** euros.

### 1200 - kritiek [n, adj] *criticism; critique; critical*

**Kritiek** leveren is makkelijker dan het ontvangen.

Offering **criticism** is easier than receiving it.

### 1201 - twaalf [num] *twelve*

Er zitten **twaalf** maanden in een jaar.
There are **twelve** months in a year.

### 1202 - spreekt [v] *to speak; to talk (2nd and 3rd person - present tense)*

Een tolk **spreekt** minstens twee talen vloeiend.
An interpreter **speaks** at least two languages fluently.

### 1203 - voorbij [adv] *finished; past*

De koets van de koning reed **voorbij**.
The King's carriage rode **past**.

### 1204 - lag [v] *to lie; to be situated (singular subjects - past tense)*

**Lag** de kat nou alweer op de koelkast?
Was the cat **lying** on top of the fridge again?

### 1205 - grens [n, v] *border; limit*

Mijn dorpje ligt vlakbij de Duitse **grens**.
My village is very close to the German **border**.

### 1206 - relatief [adj, adv] *relative(ly)*

Melk is **relatief** goedkoop hier.
Milk is **relatively** cheap here.

### 1207 - stijgen [v] *to rise; to go up (infinitive and plural subjects - present tense)*

De lift begon te **stijgen**.
The elevator started **to go up**.

**1208 - bestuurder** [n] *driver; governor*

Ik droomde over een taxi zonder **bestuurder**!
I dreamed about a taxi without a **driver**!


**1209 - gevaar** [n] *danger; risk*

Ouders zien **gevaar** eerder dan hun kinderen.
Parents see **danger** sooner than their children.

**1210 - universiteit** [n] *university*

Wat is de grootste **universiteit** in België?
What's the biggest **university** in Belgium?

**1211 - geweld** [n] *violence*

Er zit te veel **geweld** in sommige moderne films.
There's too much **violence** in some modern movies.

**1212 - maatschappij** [n] *society; company*

De antropoloog leest veel over de **maatschappij**.
The anthropologist reads a lot about **society**.

**1213 - zekerheid** [n] *certainty; security*

Zij zoekt **zekerheid** in haar relatie.
She looks for **security** in her relationship.

**1214 - wilden** [n, v] *wild ones; to want (plural subjects - past tense)*

Waarom **wilden** de schildpadden niet eten?
Why **didn't** the turtles **want** to eat?

## 1215 - politici [n] *politicians*

De **politici** maakten veel beloftes tijdens hun verkiezingscampagnes.
The **politicians** made a lot of promises during their election campaigns.

## 1216 - straat [n] *street*

Er zitten veel leuke winkels in deze **straat**.
There are a lot of nice stores on this **street**.

## 1217 - fiscale [adj, adv] *fiscal(ly); tax*

**Fiscale** paradijzen zouden niet mogen bestaan.
**Fiscal** paradises shouldn't be allowed to exist.

## 1218 - nodige [n, adj] *necessary*

Alle **nodige** ingrediënten staan in de keukenkast.
All the **necessary** ingredients are in the kitchen cupboard.

## 1219 - werkte [v] *to work (singular subjects - past tense)*

Mijn oma **werkte** vroeger op een boerderij.
My grandma used to **work** on a farm.

## 1220 - industrie [n] *industry*

Heeft hij interesse in de hout**industrie**?
Is he interested in the wood-processing **industry**?

## 1221 - voorstellen [n, v] *proposals; to propose; to introduce (infinitive and plural subjects - present tense)*

Ik zal u aan mijn man **voorstellen**.
I will **introduce** you to my husband.

### 1222 - intussen [adv] *in the meantime; meanwhile*

We zullen **intussen** vast wat drankjes bestellen.
We'll order some drinks **in the meantime**.

### 1223 - tachtig [num] *eighty*

De maximale snelheid is hier **tachtig** kilometer per uur.
The maximum speed here is **eighty** kilometers per hour.

### 1224 - handel [n, v] *store; business; wares; trade; to trade; to act (1ˢᵗ and 2ⁿᵈ person - present tense)*

De **handel** ging na dertig jaar dicht.
The **business** closed after thirty years.

### 1225 - hoort [v] *to hear; to belong (2ⁿᵈ and 3ʳᵈ person - present tense)*

**Hoort** u dat geluid ook, meneer?
Do you **hear** that sound too, sir?

### 1226 - evenwel [adv] *anyway; however; though*

Te veel taart eten is **evenwel** niet goed voor de gezondheid.
Eating too much cake isn't good for your health, **though**.

### 1227 - leiding [n] *pipe; wiring; management; leadership*

De **leiding** van de maatschappij organiseerde een spoedvergadering.
Company **management** organized an emergency meeting.

### 1228 - werkloosheid [n] *unemployment*

Is **werkloosheid** aan het stijgen of dalen?
Is **unemployment** going up or down?

**1229 - noch** [conj] *neither, nor (formal)*

De vioolspeler had **noch** honger, **noch** dorst.
The violin player was **neither** hungry **nor** thirsty.

**1230 - mate** [n] *degree; extent; moderation*

Laten we met **mate** wijn drinken.
Let's drink wine in **moderation**.

**1231 - gezicht** [n] *sight; view; face*

Ze had haar **gezicht** verbrand.
She had burned her **face**.

**1232 - interessant** [adj, adv] *interesting(ly)*

Het leven van Van Gogh was heel **interessant**.
Van Gogh's life was very **interesting**.

**1233 - vergeten** [adj, v] *forgotten; to forget (infinitive and plural subjects - present tense; past participle)*

Niet **vergeten** het licht uit te doen!
Don't **forget** to turn off the light!

**1234 - consument** [n] *consumer*

Uiteindelijk beslist de **consument**.
In the end, the **consumer** decides.

**1235 - terrein** [n] *terrain; building site; field*

Op dit **terrein** worden flats gebouwd.
Apartments will be built at this **building site**.

**1236 - sluiten** [v] *to close (infinitive and plural subjects - present tense)*

Hoe laat **sluiten** de winkels op zaterdag?

What time do the stores **close** on Saturday?

### 1237 - principe [n] *principle*

De leraar legde het **principe** van fotosynthese uit.
The teacher explained the **principle** of photosynthesis.

### 1238 - inzake [prep] *concerning*

Hij gaf antwoord **inzake** het voorstel.
He answered **concerning** the proposal.

### 1239 - overname [n] *takeover, acquisition*

Soms is een **overname** erg risicovol.
Sometimes a **takeover** is very risky.

### 1240 - beweging [n] *movement*

Die **beweging** voelt heel good.
That **movement** feels really good.

### 1241 - inflatie [n] *inflation*

Hoge **inflatie** heeft ernstige gevolgen voor de burgers.
High **inflation** has serious consequences for citizens.

### 1242 - daarin [adv] *in it/there*

Daar is de tas, doen jullie de tekeningen **daarin**?
The bag is over there, will you put the drawings **in it**?

### 1243 - wou [v] *to want (singular subjects - past tense)*

De chef **wou** een nieuw recept proberen.
The chef **wanted** to try a new recipe.

### 1244 - collectie [n] *collection*

Klaas heeft een grote **collectie** antieke boeken.
Klaas has a large **collection** of antique books.

### 1245 - verdere [adj] *further; additional*

Klik hier voor **verdere** informatie over de excursies.
Click here for **further** information about the excursions.

### 1246 - hoogste [adj] *highest*

Wat is het **hoogste** gebouw van Nederland?
What is the **highest** building in The Netherlands?

### 1247 - instellingen [n] *settings; institutions*

De programmeur kon de **instellingen** niet veranderen.
The programmer couldn't change the **settings**.

### 1248 - manager [n] *manager*

Bent u erin geïnteresseerd om **manager** te worden?
Are you interested in becoming a **manager**?

### 1249 - rekenen [v] *to calculate; to charge; to count on (infinitive and plural subjects - present tense)*

Je kan altijd op me **rekenen**!
You can always **count on** me!

### 1250 - flink [adj, adv] *robust; strong (of character); quite*

We hebben vandaag **flink** hard getraind bij crossfit.
We've trained **quite** hard at crossfit today.

### 1251 - winkels [n] *stores*

Er is uitverkoop bij de **winkels** in Arnhem!

There are sales at the **stores** in Arnhem!

**1252 - aandeelhouders** [n] *shareholders*

Hoeveel **aandeelhouders** heeft uw bedrijf?
How many **shareholders** does your company have?

**1253 - obligaties** [n] *bonds*

Hij wilde beleggen in **obligaties**.
He wanted to invest in **bonds**.

**1254 - internationaal** [adj, adv] *international*

Er is een **internationaal** zoölogie congres in Oostenrijk op twaalf oktober.
There's an **international** zoology congress in Austria on October twelfth.

**1255 - papier** [n] *paper; document*

Ga je dat **papier** recyclen?
Are you going to recycle that **paper**?

**1256 - haalde** [v] *to bring; to get; to manage to achieve something (singular subjects - past tense)*

Gisteren **haalde** onze moeder friet voor ons.
Yesterday our mother **got** French fries for us.

**1257 - ware** [adj] *true*

Psychopaten tonen niet makkelijk hun **ware** persoonlijkheid.
Psychopaths don't show their **true** personality easily.

**1258 - trekt** [v] *to pull; to hike: to attract (2<sup>nd</sup> and 3<sup>rd</sup> person - present tense)*

Het Anne Frank Huis **trekt** veel bezoekers.

The Anne Frank House **attracts** a lot of visitors.

### 1259 - bereikt [v] *to reach (2ⁿᵈ and 3ʳᵈ person - present tense)*

Dit radiogramma **bereikt** veel mensen.
This radio program **reaches** a lot of people.

### 1260 - alsof [conj] *as if/though*

Het lijkt **alsof** het gaat stormen.
It seems **as though** there's going to be a storm.

### 1261 - Belgen [n] *Belgians*

Ongeveer zestig procent van de **Belgen** spreekt Nederlands.
About sixty percent of **Belgians** speak Dutch.

### 1262 - neer [adv] *down*

Laten we op en **neer** springen!
Let's jump up and **down**!

### 1263 - karakter [n] *character*

Mijn beste vriendin heeft een heel zacht **karakter**.
My best friend has a very gentle **character**.

### 1264 - uitsluitend [adv] *exclusively*

Deze WC is **uitsluitend** voor gehandicapte mensen.
This bathroom is **exclusively** for disabled people.

### 1265 - wijst [v] *to indicate; to point (2ⁿᵈ and 3ʳᵈ person - present tense)*

The gids **wijst** naar de aap in de boom.
The guide **points** at the monkey in the tree.

**1266 - schrijft** [v] *to write (2<sup>nd</sup> and 3<sup>rd</sup> person - present tense)*

De journalist **schrijft** over Zuid-Amerika.
The journalist **writes** about South America.

**1267 - tonen** [n, v] *notes; tones; to show (infinitive and plural subjects - present tense)*

De Nigeriaanse documentaires **tonen** de realiteit van het land.
The Nigerian documentaries **show** the reality of the country.

**1268 - provincie** [n] *province, district*

Gelderland is de grootste **provincie** van Nederland.
Gelderland is the biggest **province** in The Netherlands.

**1269 - generatie** [n] *generation*

Haar ouders zijn allebei eerste-**generatie**-migranten.
Her parents are both first-**generation** immigrants.

**1270 - sneller** [adj, adv] *faster*

Het internet wordt steeds **sneller**.
The Internet is becoming **faster** and **faster**.

**1271 - hield** [v] *to hold; to keep; to continue (singular subjects - past tense)*

Gijs **hield** al zijn oude foto's in een doos.
Gijs **kept** all of his old photos in a box.

**1272 - probeert** [v] *to try (2<sup>nd</sup> and 3<sup>rd</sup> person - present tense)*

De haai **probeert** uit het net te ontsnappen.
The shark **tries** to escape from the net.

### 1273 - federale [adj] *federal*

Brussel is de **federale** hoofdstad van België.
Brussels is the **federal** capital of Belgium.

### 1274 - rug [n] *back; mountain ridge*

Yoga doen is heel goed voor je **rug**.
Doing yoga is very good for your **back**.

### 1275 - films [n] *movies; tapes*

*Flodder* is één van de populairste Nederlandse **films** ooit.
*Flodder* is one of the most popular Dutch **movies** ever.

### 1276 - discussie [n] *discussion; debate*

Er was een hevige **discussie** tussen de politici.
There was a fierce **debate** between the politicians.

### 1277 - perfect [adj, adv] *perfect(ly)*

Niemand is **perfect**!
Nobody is **perfect**!

### 1278 - sociaal [adj, adv] *sociable; social(ly)*

Tieners zijn niet per se **sociaal**.
Teenagers aren't **sociable** by definition.

### 1279 - deur [n] *door*

Die **deur** is van hout gemaakt.
That **door** is made of wood.

### 1280 - wegens [prep] *because of, due to*

De voetbalwedstrijd werd afgelast **wegens** slecht weer.
The soccer match was canceled **due to** bad weather.

**1281 - slechte** [adj] *bad; mean*

Veel boeren kampten met een **slechte** oogst dit jaar.
Many farmers struggled with a **bad** harvest this year.

**1282 - beslist** [adj, adv, v] *definitive(ly); absolutely; to decide (2ⁿᵈ and 3ʳᵈ person - present tense; past participle)*

De pasgetrouwden hadden niet **beslist** of ze kinderen wilden.
The newlyweds hadn't **decided** if they wanted children.

**1283 - dicht** [adj, adv, v] *dense; closed, shut; to write poetry (singular subjects - present tense)*

De deur moet **dicht** blijven vanwege de kou.
The door has to stay **shut** because of the cold.

**1284 - vroegere** [adj] *earlier*

Ik vind de **vroegere** albums van The Beatles de beste.
I think the Beatles' **earlier** albums are the best.

**1285 - opgericht** [v] *founded (past participle)*

Radiozender Radio 538 werd in 1992 **opgericht**.
Radio station Radio 538 was **founded** in 1992.

**1286 - vijftien** [num] *fifteen*

De ruiter had al **vijftien** medailles gewonnen.
The jockey had already won **fifteen** medals.

**1287 - stelde voor** [v] *to propose; to imagine; to introduce (singular subjects - past tense)*

Het meisje **stelde** zich **voor** hoe de vakantie ging worden.
The girl **imagined** how the holidays would turn out.

### 1288 - p [n] *the letter P*

Welke steden beginnen met een **p**?
Which cities start with a **P**?

### 1289 - alvast [adv] *in advance; in the meantime*

Kunnen jullie **alvast** een taxi bellen?
Can you call a taxi **in the meantime**?

### 1290 - vervangen [adj, v] *replaced; to replace (infinitive and plural subjects - present tense)*

We moeten de stofzuigerzak **vervangen**.
We have to **replace** the hoover bag.

### 1291 - blijken [v] *to seem; to become apparent; to turn out (infinitive and plural subjects - present tense)*

Nederlandse werkwoorden **blijken** redelijk regelmatig te zijn.
Dutch verbs **seem** to be fairly regular.

### 1292 - daling [n] *fall; descent*

Het vliegtuig start de **daling**.
The airplane starts its **descent**.

### 1293 - stemmen [v] *voices; to tune; to vote; to put in a certain mood (infinitive and plural subjects - present tense)*

**Stemmen** jouw grootouders nog steeds?
Do your grandparents still **vote**?

### 1294 - niks [n, v] *nothing (informal); to do nothing (1st and 2nd person - present tense)*

De zwerver had **niks** te eten.
The homeless man had **nothing** to eat.

**1295 - partners** [n] *partners (romantic or business)*

De **partners** van het bedrijf vierden hun grote winst.
The **partners** of the company celebrated their big profit.

**1296 - lagere** [adj] *lower*

Klaartje haalde meestal **lagere** cijfers dan Charlotte.
Klaartje usually got **lower** grades than Charlotte.

**1297 - mening** [n] *opinion*

De **mening** van de consument is belangrijk voor ons bedrijf.
The customer's **opinion** is important to our company.

**1298 - Belgisch** [adj] *Belgian*

**Belgisch** bier is wereldwijd bekend.
**Belgian** beer is famous worldwide.

**1299 - Waalse** [adj] *Walloon*

Mijn **Waalse** familie kan ook wel een beetje Nederlands.
My **Walloon** family can also speak some Dutch.

**1300 - draait** [v] *to turn; to spin around ($2^{nd}$ and $3^{rd}$ person - present tense)*

De chef **draait** de pannenkoek om.
The chef **turns** the pancake over.

**1301 - fax** [n, v] *fax; to fax ($1^{st}$ and $2^{nd}$ person - present tense)*

Ik heb al jaren geen **fax** meer gestuurd!
I haven't sent a **fax** in years!

**1302 - verplicht** [adj, adv, v] *mandatory; to oblige*

Op deze school is het **verplicht** om een uniform te dragen.
In this school, it's **mandatory** to wear a uniform.

### 1303 - vierde [n, adj] *fourth*

April is de **vierde** maand van het jaar.
April is the **fourth** month of the year.

### 1304 - tegenstelling [n] *opposition; antonym*

Een **tegenstelling** kan je ook een antoniem noemen.
You can also call an **opposition** an antonym.

### 1305 - negen [num] *nine*

Een zwangerschap duurt meestal **negen** maanden.
A pregnancy usually lasts **nine** months.

### 1306 - noodzakelijk [adj, adv] *necessary, essential(ly)*

Het is niet **noodzakelijk** om uw paspoort mee te nemen.
It's not **necessary** to take your passport.

### 1307 - auto's [n] *cars*

Elektrische **auto's** zijn beter voor het milieu.
Electric **cars** are better for the environment.

### 1308 - strategie [n] *strategy*

Wat is de beste **strategie** om een nieuwe taal te leren?
What's the best **strategy** for learning a new language?

### 1309 - verantwoordelijk [adj, adv] *responsible, responsibly*

De visagiste was **verantwoordelijk** voor de make-up van de acteurs.

The makeup artist was **responsible** for the actors' makeup.

### 1310 - geloof [n, v] *belief; to believe (1ˢᵗ and 2ⁿᵈ person - present tense)*

Ik **geloof** jouw smoesje niet!
I don't **believe** your excuse!

### 1311 - n [n] *the letter N*

Ik zei: **N**-E-E. Dus: nee!
I said: **N**-O. So: no!

### 1312 - groeien [v] *to grow (infinitive and plural subjects - present tense)*

Mijn aardbeien **groeien** goed!
My strawberries are **growing** well!

### 1313 - redenen [n] *reasons*

De directeur trad af om persoonlijke **redenen**.
The director resigned for personal **reasons**.

### 1314 - zestig [num] *sixty*

Ze nodigden **zestig** mensen uit voor hun huwelijk.
They invited **sixty** people to their wedding.

### 1315 - televisie [n, adv] *television (set)*

De **televisie** staat de hele dag aan hier.
The **television** is turned on the entire day here.

### 1316 - boodschap [n] *message; grocery*

De man kreeg een Valentijnskaart met een mooie **boodschap**.

The man received a Valentine's Day card with a beautiful **message**.

### 1317 - gebouwen [n] *buildings*

Amsterdam heeft veel prachtige **gebouwen**.
Amsterdam has a lot of beautiful **buildings**.

### 1318 - waarden [n] *values; levels*

De moeder probeert haar kinderen goede **waarden** bij te brengen.
The mother is trying to teach her children good **values**.

### 1319 - belegger [n] *investor*

Het bedrijf had nog één **belegger** nodig.
The company needed one more **investor**.

### 1320 - brief [n] *letter*

De accountant moet een belangrijke **brief** sturen.
The accountant has to send an important **letter**.

### 1321 - omstandigheden [n] *circumstances, situation*

De economische **omstandigheden** in Griekenland zijn nog steeds moeilijk.
The economic **situation** in Greece is still difficult.

### 1322 - restaurant [n] *restaurant*

Wat is het beste Indonesische **restaurant** in jouw stad?
What's the best Indonesian **restaurant** in your city?

### 1323 - historische [adj, adv] *historic(al)*

De val van de Berlijnse muur was een **historische** gebeurtenis.
The fall of the Berlin wall was a **historical** event.

### 1324 - kwartaal [n] *quarter*

In het eerste **kwartaal** van 2019 had ons bedrijf de beste resultaten.
In the first **quarter** of 2019, our company had the best results.

### 1325 - geloven [n, v] *beliefs; to believe (infinitive and plural subjects - present tense)*

Mijn kinderen **geloven** nog dat de kerstman echt is.
My children still **believe** Santa is real.

### 1326 - militaire [adj] *military*

Mijn vader heeft de **militaire** rang van kapitein.
My father has the **military** rank of captain.

### 1327 - harde [adj] *hard; tough; harsh; fast*

De band kreeg **harde** kritiek van de journalist.
The band got a **harsh** critique from the journalist.

### 1328 - kop [n] *cup; head (mostly for animals); headline; to head a ball (1$^{st}$ and 2$^{nd}$ person - present tense)*

De hamster heeft een wond op zijn **kop**.
The hamster has a wound on its **head**.

### 1329 - verbonden [n, v] *treaties; connected; bandaged (past participle)*

Deze organisatie is **verbonden** aan de Katholieke Kerk.
This organization is **connected** to the Catholic Church.

### 1330 - volk [n] *nation; people*

In een democratie kiest het **volk** politici om hun te vertegenwoordigen.
In a democracy, the **people** elect politicians to represent them.

### 1331 - aanleiding [n] *cause; reason*

De **aanleiding** voor deze spoedvergadering is ons budget.
The **reason** for this emergency meeting is our budget.

### 1332 - technologie [n] *technology*

**Technologie** veroudert steeds sneller.
**Technology** is aging more and more quickly.

### 1333 - verschillen [n, v] *differences; to differ (infinitive and plural subjects - present tense)*

Zijn er veel **verschillen** tussen Nederlands en Duits?
Are there many **differences** between Dutch and German?

### 1334 - economisch [adj, adv] *economic(ally)*

Adam Smith legde de grondbeginselen voor het **economisch** liberalisme.
Adam Smith laid the foundations for **economic** liberalism.

### 1335 - voormalige [adj] *previous, former*

De **voormalige** burgemeester was populairder dan de huidige.
The **previous** mayor was more popular than the current one.

### 1336 - beschikt [v] *to determine; to have at one's disposal (2ⁿᵈ and 3ʳᵈ person - present tense; past participle)*

De school **beschikt** over een projector en goede speakers.
The school **has** a projector and good speakers **at its disposal**.

### 1337 - elementen [n] *elements; components*

Aarde, water, vuur en lucht zijn de vier **elementen** van de natuur.
Earth, wind, fire, and air are the four **elements** of nature.

### 1338 - investering [n] *investment*

Dit huis was een goede **investering**.
This house was a good **investment**.

### 1339 - verdwijnen [v] *to disappear (infinitive and plural subjects - present tense)*

Die theevlekken **verdwijnen** gewoon in de zon.
Those tea stains will just **disappear** in the sun.

### 1340 - krant [n] *newspaper*

Mijn neef werkt voor de lokale **krant**.
My cousin works for the local **newspaper**.

### 1341 - samenleving [n] *society*

De Nederlandse **samenleving** wordt als vrij egalitair beschouwd.
Dutch **society** is considered quite egalitarian.

### 1342 - keren [n, v] *repetitions; to turn (over/around) (infinitive and plural subjects - present tense)*

Kunt u deze auto **keren**?
Could you **turn** this car around?

### 1343 - bod [n] *bid, offer*

Wij willen u graag een interessant **bod** doen.
We would like to make you an interesting **offer**.

### 1344 - vandaar [adv] *from there; that's why*

De acupuncturiste was ziek, **vandaar** dat ze er niet is.
The acupuncturist was ill, **that's why** she isn't here.

### 1345 - afdeling [n] *department; ward*

Ik zal u doorverbinden met de **afdeling** klantenservice.

I'll put you through to the customer service **department**.

### 1346 - gebeurde [v] *to happen (singular subjects - past tense)*

En wat **gebeurde** er daarna?
And what **happened** next?

### 1347 - nacht [n] *night*

Kom op, de **nacht** is nog jong!
Come on, the **night** is still young!

### 1348 - visie [n] *vision*

Een bedrijfsleider moet zijn **visie** kunnen overdragen.
A manager has to be able to transmit his **vision**.

### 1349 - rechtstreeks [adj, adv] *direct(ly)*

Deze vlucht gaat **rechtstreeks** van Amsterdam naar Toronto.
The flight goes **directly** from Amsterdam to Toronto.

### 1350 - wind [n, v] *wind; to wind (1st and 2nd person - present tense)*

De **wind** komt uit het oosten.
The **wind** is coming from the east.

### 1351 - dacht [v] *to think (singular subjects - past tense)*

Hij **dacht** dat ik Celine heette.
He **thought** my name was Celine.

### 1352 - ongetwijfeld [adv] *undoubtedly*

Rustig maar, je examen zal **ongetwijfeld** goed gaan.
Stay calm, your exam will **undoubtedly** go well.

### 1353 - leek [n, v] *layman; to seem (singular subjects - past tense)*

Het examen **leek** makkelijker dan het was.

The exam **seemed** easier than it was.

### 1354 - initiatief [n] *initiative*

Als manager zoek ik medewerkers die **initiatief** tonen.

As a manager, I'm looking for employees that show **initiative**.

### 1355 - pers [n, v] *press; Persian person; to press (1st and 2nd person - present tense)*

Er was veel **pers** aanwezig bij de filmpremière.

There was a lot of **press** present at the movie premiere.

### 1356 - kleinere [adj] *smaller*

De grote blokken zijn voor de **kleinere** kinderen.

The big blocks are for the **smaller** children.

### 1357 - eigenaar [n] *owner*

Ons lievelingsrestaurant heeft een nieuwe **eigenaar.**

Our favorite restaurant has a new **owner.**

### 1358 - structuur [n] *structure; composition*

Er bestaat een standaard**structuur** voor scripties.

There is a standard **structure** for dissertations.

### 1359 - trends [n] *trends*

Veel mensen volgen de laatste **trends** via online mode-vloggers.

Many people follow the latest **trends** through online fashion vloggers.

## 1360 - omwille [adv] *for the sake of*

Ik zal beleefd zijn **omwille** van de goede verhoudingen.
I will be polite **for the sake of** good relations.

## 1361 - waarvoor [adv] *for which; what for*

**Waarvoor** zijn deze medicijnen?
**What** is this medication **for**?

## 1362 - zelden [adv] *seldom(ly)*

Peter leest **zelden** een boek.
Peter **seldom** reads a book.

## 1363 - taak [n] *task; duty; chore*

De kaartjes controleren is jouw **taak**.
Checking the tickets is your **duty**.

## 1364 - burgemeester [n] *mayor*

De **burgemeester** zal morgen officieel het nieuwe stadshuis inhuldigen.
The **mayor** will officially inaugurate the new town hall tomorrow.

## 1365 - waard [n, adj] *male duck; innkeeper; worth*

Een bezoek aan het Rijksmuseum is iedere cent **waard**!
A visit to the Rijksmuseum is **worth** every cent!

## 1366 - klinkt [v] *to toast; to sound (2nd and 3rd person - present tense)*

Dat liedje **klinkt** me bekend in de oren.
The song **sounds** familiar to me.

## 1367 - f [n] *the letter F*

Zij wonen in flat 12**F**.

They live in apartment 12**F**.

### 1368 - daarentegen [conj] *however; on the contrary*

Mijn Duits is prima, mijn Nederlands **daarentegen** nog niet.
My German is fine, my Dutch, **however**, not yet.

### 1369 - openbare [adj] *public*

Word vandaag lid van de **openbare** bibliotheek!
Become a member of the **public** library today!

### 1370 - firma [n] *firm*

Deze **firma** produceert plastic meubels.
This **firm** produces plastic furniture.

### 1371 - tevreden [adj, adv] *satisfied*

Sorry, we waren niet **tevreden** over uw service.
Sorry, we weren't **satisfied** with your service.

### 1372 - daarop [adv] *on/to that; after*

Ze weet niet wat ze **daarop** moet antwoorden.
She doesn't know what to say **to that**.

### 1373 - behoort [v] *to belong (2nd and 3rd person - present tense)*

Deze portemonnee **behoort** tot de gast van kamer vierhondernegenenvijftig.
This wallet **belongs** to the guest from room four-hundred-fifty-nine.

### 1374 - vonden [v] *to find; to think (opinion) (plural subjects - past tense)*

De kinderen **vonden** de tekenfilm geweldig.

The children **thought** the cartoon was amazing.

### 1375 - soldaten [n] *soldiers*

De **soldaten** stonden vroeg op.
The **soldiers** got up early.

### 1376 - groeit [v] *to grow; to develop (2nd and 3rd person - present tense)*

Geld **groeit** niet op de rug!
Money doesn't grow on trees!

### 1377 - milieu [n] *environment*

Omwille het **milieu** moeten we onze $CO_2$-uitstoot verminderen.
For the sake of the **environment**, we have to reduce our $CO_2$ emissions.

### 1378 - voorkeur [n] *preference*

De zanger had een **voorkeur** voor donkere kleren.
The singer had a **preference** for dark clothes.

### 1379 - absoluut [adj, adv] *absolute(ly)*

Er zit **absoluut** geen melk in deze cake.
There is **absolutely** no milk in this cake.

### 1380 - wijzen [n, v] *wise people; ways; to point (infinitive and plural subjects - present tense)*

**Wijzen** jullie allemaal naar het Zuiderkruis?
Will you all **point** at the Southern Cross?

### 1381 - fabriek [n] *factory*

Deze **fabriek** vervuilt het rivierwater.
This **factory** is polluting the river water.

### 1382 - financieel [adj, adv] *financial(ly)*

De bejaarde man had **financieel** advies nodig.
The retired man needed **financial** advice.

### 1383 - bang [adj, adv] *afraid; scary*

De hond is **bang** voor het vuurwerk.
The dog is **afraid** of the fireworks.

### 1384 - eenmaal [adv] *once*

U moet de abonnementskosten **eenmaal** per jaar betalen.
You must pay the subscription fees **once** a year.

### 1385 - beurt [n, v] *turn, to receive money (2nd and 3rd person - present tense)*

Is het jouw **beurt**?
Is it your **turn**?

### 1386 - bewijzen [n, v] *evidence; to prove (infinitive and plural subjects - present tense)*

Onze advocaten **bewijzen** dat we onschuldig zijn.
Our lawyers **prove** that we're innocent.

### 1387 - fusie [n] *fusion, merger*

Hoe is die **fusie** tot stand gekomen?
How did the **merger** come about?

### 1388 - verantwoordelijkheid [n] *responsibility*

Kan hij de **verantwoordelijkheid** aan?
Can he handle the **responsibility**?

### 1389 - w [n] *the letter W*

Ze vond de **w** gek klinken in het Nederlands.
She thought the **W** sounded funny in Dutch.

### 1390 - sturen [v] *to steer; to send (infinitive and plural subjects - present tense)*

Mijn oom en tante **sturen** me vaak foto's van hun reizen.
My aunt and uncle often **send** me postcards of their travels.

### 1391 - ondertussen [adv] *while, in the meantime*

Gijs was aan het koken en **ondertussen** vouwde Dora de kleren op.
Gijs was cooking and **in the meantime**, Dora was folding clothes.

### 1392 - bewust [adj, adv] *previous; conscious(ly); aware of*

De schooldirecteur was zich niet **bewust** van de situatie.
The principal wasn't **aware** of the situation.

### 1393 - voortaan [adv] *from now on*

Hij besloot **voortaan** met de fiets naar zijn werk te gaan.
He decided to go to work on his bike **from now on**.

### 1394 - munt [n, v] *mint; coin; to mint (singular subjects - present tense)*

De piraat vond een enorme gouden **munt**.
The pirate found an enormous golden **coin**.

### 1395 - werkelijkheid [n] *reality*

Het Nepalese boek gaf een goed beeld van de **werkelijkheid** van het land.

The Nepalese book portrayed the country's **reality** well.

### 1396 - zekere [adj] *secure; certain*

Er is een **zekere** meneer Holmes aan de deur.
There's a **certain** Mister Holmes at the door.

### 1397 - leider [n] *leader*

Kijk jij op tegen onze **leider**?
Do you admire our **leader**?

### 1398 - rapport [n] *report (card)*

Het **rapport** is nog niet af.
The **report** isn't finished yet.

### 1399 - wegen [n, v] *roads; to weigh (infinitive and plural subjects - present tense)*

Er zijn veel files op de **wegen**.
There are many traffic jams on the **roads**.

### 1400 - onmogelijk [adj, adv] *impossible*

Nederlandse woorden goed uitspreken lijkt soms **onmogelijk**.
To pronounce Dutch words correctly sometimes seems **impossible**.

### 1401 – collega's [n] *coworkers*

Haar **collega's** organiseerden een leuk afscheidsfeestje.
Her **coworkers** organised a nice leaving party.

### 1402 - plus [n, conj] *plus; pro*

Vloeiend Spaans is een **plus** voor deze baan.
Fluent Spanish is a **plus** for this job.

**1403 - positieve** [adj] *positive*

Je komt heel ver met een **positieve** houding.
You can get very far with a **positive** attitude.

**1404 - gebouwd** [adj, v] *built (past participle)*

Wanneer zijn de Rotterdamse Kubuswoningen **gebouwd**?
When were the Rotterdam Cube Homes **built**?

**1405 - investeren** [v] *to invest (infinitive and plural subjects - present tense)*

De Japanse firma wil in ons bedrijf **investeren**.
The Japanese firm wants to **invest** in our company.

**1406 - optreden** [n, v] *performance; to occur; to perform (infinitive and plural subjects - present tense)*

Hoe laat loopt het **optreden** af?
What time will the **performance** end?

**1407 - liep** [v] *to walk; to function (singular subjects - past tense)*

De schildpad **liep** langzamer dan de haas.
The tortoise **walked** more slowly than the hare.

**1408 - boekjaar** [n] *fiscal year*

Hebben we dit **boekjaar** veel belasting betaald?
Have we paid a lot of taxes this **fiscal year**?

**1409 - werkgelegenheid** [n] *employment opportunities*

Is er veel **werkgelegenheid** in Zuid-Afrika?
Are there a lot of **employment opportunities** in South Africa?

**1410 - koop** [n, v] *purchase; to buy (1ˢᵗ and 2ⁿᵈ person -*

Hoeveel paar nieuwe schoenen **koop** je ieder jaar?
How many new pairs of shoes do you **buy** every year?

### 1411 - beschouwd [v] *considered (past participle)*

Boeren wordt als onbeleefd **beschouwd**.
To burp is **considered** impolite.

### 1412 - inwoners [n] *inhabitants*

Dit dorp heeft vierduizend **inwoners**.
This village has four thousand **inhabitants**.

### 1413 - vakbonden [n] *trade unions*

**Vakbonden** kunnen veel bereiken voor hun leden.
**Trade unions** can achieve a lot for their members.

### 1414 - inkomen [n] *income*

Heeft zij als freelancer een stabiel **inkomen**?
Does she, as a freelancer, have a stable **income**?

### 1415 - besluit [n, v] *decision; to decide (singular subjects - present tense)*

Mijn man kon geen **besluit** nemen over het cadeau.
My husband couldn't **decide** about the present.

### 1416 - dossier [n] *file*

Dit is het medisch **dossier** van mevrouw Kool.
This is Mrs. Kool's medical **file**.

### 1417 - besloten [adj, v] *private; decided (plural subjects - past tense; past participle)*

De muzikanten **besloten** het liedje te herhalen.

The musicians **decided** to repeat the song.

### 1418 - blz. [n] *abbreviation for "bladzijde", meaning page (p.)*

Het diagram staat op **blz.** 53.
The diagram is on **p.** 53.

### 1419 - beneden [adv, prep] *downstairs; below*

De katten zijn **beneden**.
The cats are **downstairs**.

### 1420 - hangen [v] *to hang (on/out) (infinitive and plural subjects - present tense)*

De jassen **hangen** aan de kapstok.
The coats **are hanging** on the coat rack.

### 1421 - geregeld [adv, v] *regularly; organized, arranged (past participle)*

Onze kinderen gaan **geregeld** naar het zwembad.
Our children go to the swimming pool **regularly**.

### 1422 - grenzen [n, v] *borders, limits; to border (infinitive and plural subjects - present tense)*

Je moet beter worden in het stellen van **grenzen**!
You have to get better at setting **boundaries**!

### 1423 - binnenkort [adv] *soon, shortly*

We gaan **binnenkort** op zakenreis.
We are going on a business trip **soon**.

### 1424 - aankoop [n] *purchase*

De **aankoop** is geregeld.

The **purchase** has been arranged.

### 1425 - huizen [n, v] *houses; to house (infinitive and plural subjects - present tense)*

De **huizen** in deze buurt hebben prachtige tuinen.
The **houses** in this neighborhood have beautiful gardens.

### 1426 - gerecht [n] *dish; court of justice*

Dit Peruaanse **gerecht** is heerlijk!
This Peruvian **dish** is delicious!

### 1427 - rijk [n, adj, adv] *state; realm; kingdom; rich(ly); copious*

De man was erg **rijk** geworden met zijn investeringen.
The man got very **rich** from his investments.

### 1428 - behouden [adj, v] *safe; to keep, to maintain (infinitive and plural subjects - present tense)*

De boten **behouden** hun koers.
The boats **are keeping** their course.

### 1429 - vlees [n] *meat*

Victoria eet sinds 2001 geen **vlees** meer.
Victoria hasn't eaten **meat** since 2001.

### 1430 - begrip [n] *understanding*

Mijn lerares toonde veel **begrip** voor mijn situatie.
My teacher showed a lot of **understanding** for my situation.

### 1431 - zeg [n] *to say; to mean (1$^{st}$ and 2$^{nd}$ person - present tense)*

**Zeg** jij vaak genoeg nee?

Do you **say** "no" often enough?

### 1432 - draaien [v] *to turn around, to spin around (infinitive and plural subjects - present tense)*

Laten we allemaal rondjes **draaien**, kinderen!
Let's all **spin** in circles, children!

### 1433 - haast [n, adv, v] *haste, hurry; almost; to rush (singular subjects - present tense)*

Het meisje kwam **haast** te laat voor haar interview!
The girl was **almost** late for her interview!

### 1434 - zette [v] *to put (singular subjects - past tense)*

De moeder **zette** de pizza op de tafel.
The mother **put** the pizza on the table.

### 1435 - zoekt [v] *to search (2ⁿᵈ and 3ʳᵈ person - present tense)*

De jongen **zoekt** een bepaald soort schaatsen.
The boy **is searching** for a certain type of ice skates.

### 1436 - gevolgd [adj, v] *followed (past participle)*

Het hert werd **gevolgd** door een jaguar.
The deer was **followed** by a jaguar.

### 1437 - daarover [adv] *about that*

Ik mag niets **daarover** zeggen.
I can't say anything **about that**.

### 1438 - overtuigd [adj, v] *convinced (past participle)*

De kinderen waren niet **overtuigd** van de goocheltruc.
The children weren't **convinced** by the magic trick.

**1439 - houding** [n] *posture; attitude*

Die kerel heeft een slechte **houding**.
That guy has a bad **attitude**.

**1440 - zeventig** [num] *seventy*

Hoe voelt het om **zeventig** te worden?
How does it feel to turn **seventy**?

**1441 - lijst** [n] *list; (picture) frame*

Hier is de **lijst** met boodschappen.
Here's the **list** of groceries.

**1442 - aarde** [n] *Earth; soil*

Mount Everest is de hoogste berg op **aarde**.
Mount Everest is the highest mountain on **Earth**.

**1443 - blad** [n] *leaf; sheet; magazine; serving tray*

Zie je die rups op het **blad**?
Do you see that caterpillar on the **leaf**?

**1444 - gestegen** [adj, v] *risen, gone up (past participle)*

De olieprijzen zijn flink **gestegen**.
Oil prices have **risen** sharply.

**1445 - normaal** [adj, adv] *normal(ly)*

Uw bloeddruk is niet **normaal**.
Your blood pressure isn't **normal**.

**1446 - eindelijk** [adv] *finally*

Frits heeft **eindelijk** zijn rijexamen gehaald.
Frits **finally** passed his driving test.

**1447 - operatie** [n] *operation*

Mevrouw, uw dochters **operatie** is geslaagd.
Ma'am, your daughter's **operation** was a success.

**1448 - verlaten** [adj, v] *abandoned; to leave (infinitive and plural subjects - present tense; past participle)*

Dat huis ziet er **verlaten** uit.
That house looks **abandoned**.

**1449 - zomaar** [adv] *for no reason*

Ze kocht **zomaar** een cadeau voor haar moeder.
She bought a present for a mother **for no reason**.

**1450 - fout** [n, adj, adv] *mistake; incorrect(ly)*

Helaas, dat antwoord is **fout**.
Unfortunately, that answer is **incorrect**.

**1451 - verdienen** [v] *to earn; to deserve (infinitive and plural subjects - present tense)*

De stagiaires **verdienen** geen geld, maar doen wel ervaring op.
The interns don't **earn** any money, but are getting experience.

**1452 - belastingen** [n] *taxes; loads*

Wat voor **belastingen** moeten bedrijven betalen?
What kinds of **taxes** do companies have to pay?

**1453 - straks** [adv] *soon; later*

We zien jullie **straks**.
We'll see you **later**.

**1454 - behoefte** [n] *need; requirement*

Ze had geen **behoefte** aan hulp.

She didn't have a **need** for help.

### 1455 - trok [v] *to pull; to hike; to attract (singular subjects - past tense)*

De hond **trok** aan het tafelkleed.
The dog **pulled** the tablecloth.

### 1456 - verhalen [v] *stories; to tell (infinitive and plural subjects - present tense)*

Schrijfster Annie M.G. Schmidt heeft prachtige **verhalen** voor kinderen geschreven.
Author Annie M.G. Schmidt has written beautiful **stories** for children.

### 1457 - elders [adv] *elsewhere*

Voor kampeeruitrusting moet u **elders** zijn.
You'll have to go **elsewhere** for camping equipment.

### 1458 - snelle [adj] *quick, fast*

De architect maakte een **snelle** schets van het project.
The architect made a **quick** sketch of the project.

### 1459 - duizenden [n] *thousands*

Ieder jaar gaan er **duizenden** mensen naar het Lowlands Festival.
Every year, **thousands** of people go to the Lowlands Festival.

### 1460 - elektronische [adj] *electronic*

De **elektronische** tickets werden gescand.
The **electronic** tickets were scanned.

### 1461 - weliswaar [adv] *indeed; admittedly*

Het is **weliswaar** zonnig, maar niet zo warm.

It is **indeed** sunny, but not very warm.

### 1462 - interessante [adj] *interesting*

Morgen is er een **interessante** film op kanaal 5.
Tomorrow there will be an **interesting** movie on channel 5.

### 1463 - pond [n] *metric pound; pound sterling*

Een **pond** belegen kaas, alstublieft.
One **pound** of mature cheese, please.

### 1464 - verhouding [n] *proportion; relationship; love affair*

De **verhouding** tussen de torso en de benen klopt niet.
The **proportion** between the torso and legs isn't right.

### 1465 - dreigt [v] *to threaten; to loom (2nd and 3rd person - present tense)*

Er **dreigt** groot gevaar hier.
Great danger **looms** here.

### 1466 - modellen [n] *models*

Deze kleren zijn voor de **modellen**.
These clothes are for the **models**.

### 1467 - kwijt [adj] *lost*

Ben je je sleutels weer **kwijt**?
Have you **lost** your keys again?

### 1468 - koersen [n] *(exchange) rate; value; course*

De internationale **koersen** bleven stabiel afgelopen september.
International **exchange rates** stayed stable last September.

**1469 - vrijheid** [n] *freedom; liberty*

Iedereen is op zoek naar **vrijheid**.
Everyone is in search of **freedom**.

**1470 - individuele** [adj] *individual*

Alle passagiers kregen een **individuele** portie taart.
All passengers got an **individual** portion of cake.

**1471 - behoorlijk** [adj, adv] *decent; quite*

Dit boek over belastingen is **behoorlijk** saai.
This book about taxes is **quite** boring.

**1472 - marketing** [n] *marketing*

In **marketing** investeren is ongelofelijk belangrijk.
Investing in **marketing** is incredibly important.

**1473 - belasting** [n] *tax; duty; load*

Hoe meer je verdient, hoe meer **belasting** je betaalt.
The more you earn, the more **tax** you pay.

**1474 - veertig** [num] *forty*

Dat is dan drie euro **veertig**.
That'll be three euro **forty**.

**1475 - reclame** [n] *advertisement; commercials*

**Reclame** op TV kan heel irritant zijn.
**Commercials** on TV can be very annoying.

**1476 - liter** [n] *liter*

We moeten één **liter** water per persoon meenemen.
We have to take one **liter** of water per person.

211

### 1477 - meisjes [n] *(little) girls*

**Meisjes** aan deze kant, jongens aan die kant.
**Girls** on this side, boys on that side.

### 1478 - honderden [n] *hundreds*

Er vlogen **honderden** zeemeeuwen langs.
**Hundreds** of seagulls flew by.

### 1479 - officieel [adj, adv] *official(ly)*

Deze informatie is nog niet **officieel**.
This information isn't **official** yet.

### 1480 - aangeboden [v] *offered (past participle)*

De blinde man kreeg hulp **aangeboden**.
The blind man was **offered** help.

### 1481 - gelegenheid [n] *opportunity; occasion; public place*

Babette kocht een jurk voor een speciale **gelegenheid**.
Babette bought a dress for a special **occasion**.

### 1482 - neus [n, v] *nose; to nose around (1<sup>st</sup> and 2<sup>nd</sup> person - present tense)*

De bokser kreeg een klap op zijn **neus**.
The boxer took a blow to the **nose**.

### 1483 - fors [adj, adv] *sturdy; stocky; substantial(ly)*

De yogaleraar is **fors**, maar heel lenig.
The yoga teacher is **stocky**, but very flexible.

### 1484 - gebaseerd [v] *based (past participle)*

Is deze film **gebaseerd** op een boek?

Is this film **based** on a book?

### 1485 - verdwenen [v] *to disappear (plural subjects - past tense; past participle)*

Zijn acné was eindelijk **verdwenen**.
His acné had finally **disappeared**.

### 1486 - trend [n] *trend*

Kort haar voor meisjes is nu de nieuwste **trend**.
Short hair for girls is now the latest **trend**.

### 1487 - koning [n] *king*

**Koning** Filip werd in 2013 officieel Koning van België.
**King** Philipe officially became King of Belgium in 2013.

### 1488 - veranderd [v] *changed (past participle)*

Haar ouderlijk huis was erg weinig **veranderd**.
Her childhood home had **changed** very little.

### 1489 - concept [n] *concept*

De start-up werkt aan een nieuw **concept**.
The startup is working on a new **concept**.

### 1490 - gezin [n] *family*

In ons **gezin** wordt veel gelachen.
There's a lot of laughter in our **family**.

### 1491 - rechten [n, v] *Law; rights; to straighten (infinitive and plural subjects - present tense)*

Kent u uw **rechten**?
Do you know your **rights**?

## 1492 - winnen [v] *to win; to extract (minerals) (infinitive and plural subjects - present tense)*

Ons team gaat **winnen**, ik voel het!
Our team is going to **win**, I can feel it!

## 1493 - deden [v] *to do (plural subjects - past tense)*

De gasten **deden** de afwas.
The guests **did** the dishes.

## 1494 - ergens [adv] *somewhere; with something; somewhat*

Kom, we gaan **ergens** anders zitten.
Come on, let's go and sit **somewhere** else.

## 1495 - nochtans [adv] *nevertheless; though*

Mijn schoonouders waren serieus, **nochtans** ook vriendelijk.
My parents-in-law were serious, **though** also friendly.

## 1496 - behoren [v] *to belong (infinitive and plural subjects - present tense)*

Deze zinnen **behoren** tot de vragencategorie.
These sentences **belong** to the question category.

## 1497 - kantoor [n] *office*

Ik zie je straks op **kantoor**!
I'll see you at the **office** later!

## 1498 - Nederlanders [n] *Dutch people*

Waarom spreken zoveel **Nederlanders** zo goed Engels?
Why do so many **Dutch people** speak English so well?

## 1499 - dienen [v] *to serve; ought to (infinitive and plural*

*subjects - present tense)*

De leerlingen **dienen** op tijd in de klas te zijn.

The students **ought to** be in their classrooms on time.

### 1500 - bijkomende [adj] *additional; collateral*

Het ongeluk veroorzaakte veel **bijkomende** schade.

The accident caused a lot of **collateral** damage.

### 1501 - hoopt [v] *to hope (2ⁿᵈ and 3ʳᵈ person - present tense)*

De chirurg **hoopt** op een goede afloop.

The surgeon **is hoping** for a good result.

### 1502 - tijden [n] *times; verb tenses*

Vandaag oefenen we alle tegenwoordige **tijden**.

Today we'll practice all present **tenses**.

### 1503 - kijkt [v] *to look; to watch (2ⁿᵈ and 3ʳᵈ person - present tense)*

Het publiek **kijkt** vol hoop naar de paardenrace.

The audience **is watching** the horse race full of hope.

### 1504 - campagne [n] *campaign*

De politicus investeerde veel in zijn politieke **campagne**.

The politician invested a lot in his political **campaign**.

### 1505 - jaarlijkse [adj] *yearly*

Het **jaarlijkse** bloemencorso is aankomend weekend.

The **yearly** flower parade is this weekend.

**1506 - glas** [n] *glass*

Is het **glas** halfvol of half leeg?
Is the **glass** half full or half empty?

**1507 - beurzen** [n] *wallets; scholarships; fairs; stock exchanges*

De **beurzen** wankelen na de terroristische aanslag.
The **stock exchanges** are reeling after the terrorist attack.

**1508 - rechter** [n, adj] *judge; straighter*

De verdachte werd schuldig verklaard door de **rechter**.
The suspect was declared guilty by the **judge**.

**1509 - sectoren** [n] *sectors*

Twee **sectoren** van de kernreactor zijn onveilig.
Two of the **sectors** of the nuclear reactor are unsafe.

**1510 - verklaring** [n] *statement; declaration; explanation*

Ze vonden geen **verklaring** voor de graancirkels.
They couldn't find an **explanation** for the crop circles.

**1511 - bedroeg** [v] *to amount to (singular subjects - past tense)*

Uiteindelijk **bedroeg** het totaal vierendertig euro.
In the end, the total **amounted to** thirty-four euros.

**1512 - aangepast** [v] *tried on; adapted (past participle)*

De planning is zojuist **aangepast**.
The planning has just been **adapted**.

**1513 - analisten** [n] *analysts*

De **analisten** schreven een rapport met hun prognoses.

The **analysts** wrote a report with their forecasts.

### 1514 - feite [n] *almost exclusively used in the set expression "in feite", meaning in fact; practically*

Hij heeft in **feite** het huis voor zichzelf.
He **practically** has the house to himself.

### 1515 - opzichte [n] *almost exclusively used in the set expression "ten opzichte van", meaning regarding; compared to*

Ten **opzichte** van vorig jaar heeft hij het dit jaar drukker.
**Compared to** last year, he's busier this year.

### 1516 - tientallen [n] *tens of, dozens*

Er kwamen **tientallen** sollicitatie-e-mails binnen.
**Dozens** of email applications came in.

### 1517 - auteur [n] *author*

Haar favoriete **auteur** was Remco Campert.
Her favorite **author** was Remco Campert.

### 1518 - traditie [n] *tradition*

Pannenkoeken eten met kaas en stroop is een typisch Nederlandse **traditie**.
Eating pancakes with cheese and sugar syrup is a typically Dutch **tradition**.

### 1519 - westerse [adj] *Western*

In **westerse** landen worden meer producten geconsumeerd.
In **Western** countries, more products are being consumed.

### 1520 - bureau [n] *desk; (police) office*

Het **bureau** ligt vol met boeken.

The **desk** is full of books.

### 1521 - behalve [conj] *except*

Iedereen **behalve** Beatrix had de autogordel om.

Everyone **except** Beatrix was wearing their seatbelt.

### 1522 - automatisch [adj, adv] *automatical(ly)*

Het licht ging **automatisch** aan!

The lights went on **automatically**!

### 1523 - pakken [n, v] *boxes; suits; to catch; to get; to pack; to dupe (infinitive and plural subjects - present tense)*

Wie gaat de borden **pakken**?

Who's going to **get** the plates?

### 1524 - vermijden [v] *to avoid, to evade (infinitive and plural subjects - present tense)*

De autistische jongens **vermijden** drukke plaatsen.

The autistic boys **avoid** busy places.

### 1525 - uren [n] *hours*

Mijn tatoeage laten zetten duurde **uren**!

Getting my tattoo took **hours**!

### 1526 - beschikken [v] *to determine; to have at one's disposal (infinitive and plural subjects - present tense)*

Wij **beschikken** niet over een helikopter.

We don't have a helicopter **at our disposal**.

**1527 - geraakt** [adj, v] *(emotionally) affected; hit; wounded (past participle)*

De soldaat werd **geraakt** door een kogel.
The soldier was **hit** by a bullet.

**1528 - dalen** [n, v] **valleys; *to decrease; to descend (infinitive and plural subjects - present tense)***

Het hoge waterpeil van de gracht zal vanavond **dalen**.
The high water levels of the canal will **decrease** tonight.

**1529 - draagt** [v] *to carry; to wear (2nd and 3rd person - present tense)*

De peuter **draagt** zijn eigen rugzak.
The toddler **is carrying** his own backpack.

**1530 - openbaar** [adj, adv] *public(ly)*

**Openbaar** vervoer is de meest milieuvriendelijke manier van transport.
**Public** transport is the most eco-friendly means of transport.

**1531 - Engels** [n, adj] *English (language)*

Vinden jullie **Engels** makkelijker dan Nederlands?
Do you think **English** is easier than Dutch?

**1532 - maakten** [v] *to make; to fix (plural subjects - past tense)*

De kinderen **maakten** een kaart voor hun ouders.
The children **made** a card for their parents.

**1533 - fonds** [n] *fund; trust; foundation*

De prinses had een **fonds** voor de armen opgezet.
The princess had set up a **fund** for the poor.

### 1534 - h [n] *the letter H*

In het Spaans wordt the **h** meestal niet uitgesproken.
In Spanish, **the letter H** usually isn't pronounced.

### 1535 - degelijk [adj, adv] *solid; reliable; certainly*

Die schommelstoel is heel **degelijk**.
That rocking chair is very **solid**.

### 1536 - gehaald [v] *brought; attained; managed to achieve something (past participle)*

Mijn vrienden hebben pizza **gehaald**.
My friends have **brought** pizza.

### 1537 - voet [n] *foot; base*

Ze stootte haar **voet**.
She bumped her **foot**.

### 1538 - eraan [adj] *(on) it/them*

Daar is een stoel, hang jij mijn tas **eraan**?
There's a chair, will you hang my bag **on it**?

### 1539 - stem [n, v] *voice; vote; to vote; to tune (1ˢᵗ and 2ⁿᵈ person - present tense)*

Iedere **stem** telt.
Every **vote** counts.

### 1540 - roman [n] *novel*

"De Avonden" is een prachtige klassieke Nederlandse **roman**.
"De Avonden" is a beautiful, classic Dutch **novel**.

### 1541 - uitbreiding [n] *expansion; extension*

Het restaurant plant een **uitbreiding** voor volgend jaar.

The restaurant is planning an **extension** for next year.

### 1542 - voorstelling [n] *performance; show*

De **voorstelling** begint over tien minuten.
The **show** is starting in ten minutes.

### 1543 - imago [n] *image*

Een goed **imago** is cruciaal voor filmsterren.
A good **image** is crucial for film stars.

### 1544 - tekort [n] *shortage*

Het **tekort** aan leerkrachten blijft groeien.
The **shortage** of teachers keeps growing.

### 1545 - bedragen [n, v] *amounts; to amount to (infinitive and plural subjects - present tense)*

Dat zijn forse **bedragen**.
Those are substantial **amounts**.

### 1546 - organiseert [v] *to organize (2nd and 3rd person - present tense)*

Het koor **organiseert** hun jaarlijkse kerstvoorstelling.
The choir **is organizing** its yearly Christmas show.

### 1547 - negatieve [adj] *negative*

Ik vermijd **negatieve** opmerkingen.
I avoid **negative** remarks.

### 1548 - uitspraak [n] *pronunciation; judgement*

Jullie **uitspraak** is enorm verbeterd!
Your **pronunciation** has improved enormously!

### 1549 - onderhandelingen [n] *negotiations*

De **onderhandelingen** liepen vast.
The **negotiations** collapsed.

### 1550 - zoiets [n] *something like (that)*

Ik zou nooit **zoiets** als bungeejumpen durven.
I would never dare doing **something like** bungee jumping.

### 1551 - activiteit [n] *activity*

De leraar organiseerde een leuke **activiteit**.
The teacher organized a fun **activity**.

### 1552 - goud [n] *gold*

Is die ring van zilver of **goud**?
Is that ring made of silver or **gold**?

### 1553 - type [n] *type*

Is Katja Schuurman jouw **type**?
Is Katja Schuurman your **type**?

### 1554 - beheer [n, v] *management, administration; to manage (1st and 2nd person - present tense)*

De webmaster is verantwoordelijk voor het **beheer** van de website.
The webmaster is responsible for the website **management**.

### 1555 - steken [n, v] *(sowing) stitches; stabs; to sting; to stab (infinitive and plural subjects - present tense)*

De muggen **steken** vooral in mijn kuiten.
The mosquitoes are mostly **stinging** me in my calves.

## 1556 - slachtoffer [n] *victim*

Snel, dit **slachtoffer** moet het eerst naar het ziekenhuis.
Quick, this **victim** has to go to the hospital first.

## 1557 - ontdekt [v] *to discover (2ⁿᵈ and 3ʳᵈ person - present tense; past participle)*

Newton heeft de zwaartekracht in 1664 **ontdekt**.
Newton **discovered** gravity in 1664.

## 1558 - wereldwijd [adj, adv] *worldwide*

De zanger wilde **wereldwijd** bekend worden.
The singer wanted to become famous **worldwide**.

## 1559 - goedkoper [adj] *cheaper*

Mijn nieuwe abonnement is **goedkoper** dan het vorige.
My new subscription is **cheaper** than the previous.

## 1560 - eenvoudige [adj] *plain; simple*

Deze **eenvoudige** puzzel is van mijn peuter.
This **simple** jigsaw is my toddler's.

## 1561 - betekenis [n] *meaning; significance*

De **betekenis** vind je in het woordenboek.
You'll find the **meaning** in the dictionary.

## 1562 - afgesloten [v] *closed (off) (past participle)*

Vanaf morgen wordt deze weg **afgesloten**.
Starting tomorrow, this road will be **closed off**.

## 1563 - techniek [n] *engineering; technique*

De gymnast heeft een indrukwekkende **techniek**!

The gymnast has impressive **technique**!

### 1564 - meisje [n] *(little) girl*

Het **meisje** had twee vlechtjes in.
The **girl** was wearing two braids.

### 1565 - zwart [n, adj] *black*

Zijn haar is **zwart**.
His hair is **black**.

### 1566 - stonden [v] *to stand; to be written (plural subjects - past tense)*

Er **stonden** veel mensen bij de kassa.
There were a lot of people **standing** at the cash register.

### 1567 - verandering [n] *change*

Vindt u het moeilijk om deze **verandering** te accepteren?
Do you find it hard to accept this **change**?

### 1568 - voort [adv] *on(wards); forward; ahead*

Na de onderbreking zette de leraar de les **voort**.
After the interruption, the teacher moved **forward** with the class.

### 1569 - werking [n] *operation; functioning; effect*

We begrijpen de **werking** van dit apparaat niet.
We don't understand the **operation** of this appliance.

### 1570 - beperkte [adj] *limited*

De verlegen influencer had maar een **beperkte** invloed.
The shy influencer had only **limited** influence.

### 1571 - olie [n] *oil; petrol*

De industriële sector kan momenteel niet zonder **olie**.
Industry can't exist without **oil** at the moment.

### 1572 - Vlamingen [n] *Flemish people*

De meeste **Vlamingen** spreken Vlaams, een Nederlands dialect.
The majority of **Flemish people** speak Flemish, a Dutch dialect.

### 1573 - zuiden [n] *south; southern*

Patagonië ligt in het **zuiden** van Argentinië.
Patagonia is located in the **south** of Argentina.

### 1574 - dure [adj] *expensive*

De dieven hebben hele **dure** sieraden gestolen.
The thieves have stolen very **expensive** jewelry.

### 1575 - vluchtelingen [n] *refugees*

De **vluchtelingen** hadden twee dagen niets gegeten.
The **refugees** hadn't eaten in two days.

### 1576 - schrijver [n] *writer*

Jef Geeraerts is mijn favoriete Vlaamse **schrijver**.
Jef Geeraerts is my favorite Flemish **writer**.

### 1577 - universiteiten [n] *universities*

Steeds meer **universiteiten** bieden online studies aan.
More and more **universities** are offering online courses.

### 1578 - banen [n] *jobs; tracks; stripes; runways*

Er zijn weinig nieuwe **banen** gecreëerd dit jaar.
Few new **jobs** have been created this year.

### 1579 - belangen [n] *interests*

Je moet leren om je **belangen** te verdedigen!
You have to learn to defend your **interests**!

### 1580 - georganiseerd [v] *organized (past participle)*

Mijn vader heeft een volksdansfestival **georganiseerd**.
My father has **organized** a folk dance festival.

### 1581 - duizend [num] *a thousand*

De man gaat **duizend** euro van de bank lenen.
The man is going to borrow **a thousand** euros from the bank.

### 1582 - jeugd [n] *childhood*

We hadden een moeilijke **jeugd**.
We had a difficult **childhood**.

### 1583 - verdeeld [adj, v] *divided; allocated; split (past participle)*

De koekjes zijn eerlijk **verdeeld**.
The cookies were **split** fairly.

### 1584 - gesproken [adj, v] *spoken (past participle)*

Ik heb Jan gisteren niet **gesproken**.
I haven't **spoken** to Jan yesterday.

### 1585 - publieke [adj] *public*

Werk in de **publieke** sector heeft veel voordelen.
Working in the **public** sector has many advantages.

### 1586 - gesprekken [n] *conversations*

Na veel **gesprekken** besloot het koppel te scheiden.

After many **conversations**, the couple decided to get divorced.

### 1587 - vriend [n] *friend; boyfriend*

Is Anton haar beste **vriend**?
Is Anton her best **friend**?

### 1588 - ministers [n] *ministers*

De **ministers** waren het niet eens over het voorstel.
The **ministers** disagreed about the proposal.

### 1589 - ziekte [n] *disease*

Ik heb een tropische **ziekte** opgelopen in het regenwoud.
I contracted a tropical **disease** in the rainforest.

### 1590 - onderwerp [n, v] *subject, topic; to subject to (1st and 2nd person - present tense)*

Ze kon geen **onderwerp** kiezen voor haar opstel.
She couldn't decide on a **topic** for her essay.

### 1591 - stoppen [n, v] *fuses; to mend clothes; to stop (infinitive and plural subjects - present tense)*

De auto's **stoppen** bij het stoplicht.
The cars **stop** at the traffic lights.

### 1592 - toestand [n] *condition; state*

In zijn **toestand** kan hij niet werken.
He can't work in his **condition**.

### 1593 - meent [v] *to mean; to believe (2nd and 3rd person - present tense)*

Hij **meent** het niet, het is een grapje.
He doesn't **mean** it, it's a joke.

**1594 - verklaart** [v] *to declare; to explain (2<sup>nd</sup> and 3<sup>rd</sup> person - present tense)*

Dat **verklaart** veel!
That **explains** a lot!

**1595 - kocht** [v] *to buy (singular subjects - past tense)*

De moeder **kocht** ijs voor haar familie.
The mother **bought** icecream for her family.

**1596 - hedendaagse** [adj] *present-day, contemporary*

Mijn oma vindt de **hedendaagse** muziek vreselijk!
My grandmother thinks **contemporary** music is awful!

**1597 - analyse** [n] *analysis*

Het laboratorium is bijna klaar met de **analyse**.
The laboratory is almost done with the **analysis**.

**1598 - wereldoorlog** [n] *world war*

De Tweede **Wereldoorlog** duurde zes jaar.
The Second **World War** lasted six years.

**1599 - gelegd** [v] *to put, to place (past participle)*

Ze heeft de sleutels daar **gelegd**.
She **put** the keys over there.

**1600 - richten** [v] *to aim; to focus on (infinitive and plural subjects - present tense)*

Het bedrijf gaat zich **richten** op de Amerikaanse markt.
The company is going **to focus on** the American market.

**1601 - achtergrond** [n] *background; origins*

De **achtergrond** van de tekening is nog niet af.
The **background** of the drawing isn't finished yet.

**1602 - debat** [n] *debate*

Hoe laat begint het **debat**?
What time will the **debate** start?

**1603 - vaker** [adv] *more often*

Zij gaan **vaker** naar de supermarkt dan wij.
They go to the supermarket **more often** than us.

**1604 - forse** [adj] *sturdy; stocky; large; substantial*

De rechtszaak gaat een **forse** hoeveelheid geld kosten.
The trial is going to cost a **large** amount of money.

**1605 - goederen** [n] *goods*

De **goederen** zijn aangekomen.
The **goods** have arrived.

**1606 - burgers** [n] *citizens; civilians*

De **burgers** kwamen in opstand.
The **citizens** revolted.

**1607 - hof** [n] *(royal) court; courtyard*

Er staan mooie bloemen in het **hof**.
There are beautiful flowers in the **courtyard**.

**1608 - geleid** [adj, v] *led; guided (past participle)*

De schapen werden naar het weiland **geleid**.
The sheep were **led** to the meadow.

### 1609 - gespeeld [adj, v] *played (past participle)*

De meisjes hebben leuk samen **gespeeld**.

The girls have **played** together nicely.

### 1610 - nv [n] *abbreviation for "naamloze vennootschap", meaning "limited company"*

Zou de bedrijfsnaam TwoLips **nv** al ingenomen zijn?

Do you think the company name TwoLips **Ltd.** is already taken?

### 1611 - angst [n] *fear*

Lees dit advies om die **angst** te overwinnen!

Read this advice to conquer that **fear**!

### 1612 - onderzoeken [n, v] *studies; to research; to investigate (infinitive and plural subjects - present tense)*

De bank gaat de fraude meteen **onderzoeken**.

The bank is going to **investigate** the fraud immediately.

### 1613 - schuld [n] *debt; fault*

Het was zijn **schuld**.

It was his **fault**.

### 1614 - dichter [n, adj, adv] *poet; closer*

Ken jij de **dichter** Tsead Bruinja?

Have you heard of the **poet** Tsead Bruinja?

### 1615 - afkomstig [adj] *originating/comes from*

Dit tapijt is **afkomstig** uit India.

This rug **comes from** India.

**1616 - eventuele** [adj] *possible; potential*

U kunt ons e-mailen met **eventuele** vragen.
You can email us any **possible** questions.

**1617 - kunstenaar** [n] *artist*

De accountant droomde ervan om **kunstenaar** te worden.
The accountant dreamt about becoming an **artist**.

**1618 - stijgt** [v] *to rise; to go up (2nd and 3rd person - present tense)*

Het waterpeil van de gracht **stijgt** en daalt dagelijks.
The water level of the canal **rises** and falls daily.

**1619 - college** [n] *school; board; lecture*

De professor zal op maandag haar eerste **college** geven.
The professor will give her first **lecture** on Monday.

**1620 - vuur** [n, v] *fire; to fire (1st and 2nd person - present tense)*

Naar **vuur** kijken is kalmerend.
Watching **fire** is calming.

**1621 - interne** [adj] *internal*

Het slachtoffer heeft vele **interne** verwondingen.
The victim has many **internal** injuries.

**1622 - letterlijk** [adj, adv] *literal(ly)*

Iets **letterlijk** vertalen creëert soms grappige zinnen.
Translating something **literally** sometimes creates funny sentences.

### 1623 - contacten [n] *contacts; connection*

Het is goed om zakelijke **contacten** te onderhouden.

It's good to maintain business **contacts**.

### 1624 - vrijwel [adv] *practically*

We ontbijten iedere dag **vrijwel** hetzelfde.

We have **practically** the same thing for breakfast every day.

### 1625 - kiest [v] *to choose (2nd and 3rd person - present tense)*

Geertje **kiest** meestal dezelfde muziek.

Geertje usually **chooses** the same music.

### 1626 - slaan [v] *to hit (infinitive and plural subjects - present tense)*

De timmermannen **slaan** met hun hamers op de spijkers.

The carpenters **hit** the nails with their hammers.

### 1627 - grotendeels [adv] *mostly, largely*

De verbouwing is **grotendeels** afgerond.

The renovation has **largely** been finished.

### 1628 - verwachtingen [n] *expectations*

De burgers hadden geen hoge **verwachtingen** van de nieuwe president.

The citizens didn't have high **expectations** of the new president.

### 1629 - dubbele [adj] *double*

Mag ik een **dubbele** portie friet?

Can I have a **double** portion of French fries?

### 1630 - k [n] *the letter K*

Hoeveel sporten ken je die met een **k** beginnen?
How many sports do you know that start with a **K**?

### 1631 - voert [v] *to feed (2nd and 3rd person - present tense)*

Tom **voert** de geiten 's ochtends.
Tom **feeds** the goats in the mornings.

### 1632 - rustig [adj, adv] *calm(ly)*

Blijf **rustig**, het komt goed.
Stay **calm**, things will be fine.

### 1633 - gedacht [v] *to think (past participle)*

Daar hadden ze niet aan **gedacht**.
They hadn't **thought** about that.

### 1634 - aanwezigheid [n] *presence*

Uw **aanwezigheid** wordt erg gewaardeerd.
Your **presence** is highly appreciated.

### 1635 - rechtbank [n] *court; courthouse*

De rechter en advocaten waren al in de **rechtbank**.
The judge and lawyer were already at the **courthouse**.

### 1636 - verscheen [v] *to appear; to come out; to be published (singular subjects - past tense)*

Vorige week **verscheen** de nieuwe film van Tarantino!
Tarantino's new film **came out** last week!

### 1637 - baas [n] *boss; owner of a pet*

Wie is de **baas**, jij of je kind?
Who's the **boss**, you or your child?

### 1638 - stevige [adj] *sturdy; drastic*

We zoeken een **stevige** houten tafel.
We're looking for a **sturdy** wooden table.

### 1639 - uiterst [adj, adv] *extreme(ly)*

Men moet **uiterst** voorzichtig met kwik omgaan.
One must handle mercury **extremely** carefully.

### 1640 - obligatie [n] *bond*

Wat zal het rendement van deze **obligatie** zijn?
What will be the yield of this **bond**?

### 1641 - verzet [n, v] *resistance; to resist (singular subjects - present tense)*

De ezel **verzet** zich tegen de boer die hem trekt.
The donkey **resists** the farmer that's pulling him.

### 1642 - raken [v] *to affect (emotionally); to hit; to be wounded (infinitive and plural subjects - past tense)*

De jagers gaan proberen de vos te **raken**.
The hunters are going to try to **hit** the fox.

### 1643 - volgde [v] *to follow (singular subjects - past tense)*

De hond **volgde** zijn baas.
The dog **followed** his owner.

### 1644 - reizen [n, v] *journeys; to travel (infinitive and*

De studenten **reizen** samen naar Canada.

The students **travel** to Canada together.

### 1645 - ontwerpen [n, v] *designs; to design (infinitive and plural subjects - present tense)*

Marieke vond de **ontwerpen** van Iris van Herpen innovatief.

Marieke thought Iris van Herpen's **designs** were innovative.

### 1646 - formule [n] *formula*

Eureka, ik heb de **formule** ontdekt!

Eureka, I've discovered the **formula**!

### 1647 - reageren [v] *to react; to respond (infinitive and plural subjects - present tense)*

Hoe zal je moeder op het nieuws **reageren**?

How is your mother going to **react** to the news?

### 1648 - doden [n, v] *dead; to kill (infinitive and plural subjects - present tense)*

Zombies zijn de **doden** die opeens beginnen te lopen.

Zombies are **the dead** that suddenly start walking.

### 1649 - vergadering [n] *meeting; gathering*

De **vergadering** wordt uitgesteld tot komende maandag.

The **meeting** is being postponed until Monday.

### 1650 - gebeurd [v] *happened (past participle)*

Wat is hier **gebeurd**?

What has **happened** here?

### 1651 - verkoopt [v] *to sell (2nd and 3rd person - present*

*tense)*

**Verkoopt** u ook dekbedden?
Do you also **sell** comforters?

### 1652 - gemeenschap [n] *community*

De **gemeenschap** van het dorp was erg goed georganiseerd.
The village **community** was very well-organized.

### 1653 - inbegrepen [adj] *included*

Is het ontbijt **inbegrepen**?
Is breakfast **included**?

### 1654 - diep [adj, adv] *deep; profound*

Het zwembad is twee meter **diep**.
The swimming pool is two meters **deep**.

### 1655 - regisseur [n] *director*

Paul Verhoeven is een bekende Nederlandse **regisseur** in Hollywood.
Paul Verhoeven is a well-known Dutch **director** in Hollywood.

### 1656 - natuurlijke [adj] *natural*

**Natuurlijke** middelen hebben meestal minder bijwerkingen.
**Natural** medicine usually has fewer side effects.

### 1657 - uitzondering [n] *exception*

Het hotel zal een **uitzondering** maken voor de ambassadeur.
The hotel will make an **exception** for the ambassador.

### 1658 - komst [n] *arrival; visit*

We kijken uit naar je **komst**.

We're looking forward to your **arrival**.

### 1659 - definitief [adj, adv] *definite(ly)*

Ze wilden **definitief** geen kinderen.
They **definitely** didn't want to have children.

### 1660 - werkgevers [n] *employers*

**Werkgevers** stellen eerlijkheid erg op prijs.
**Employers** highly appreciate honesty.

### 1661 - begrijpen [v] *to understand (infinitive and plural subjects - present tense)*

De rappers waren moeilijk te **begrijpen**.
The rappers were difficult to **understand**.

### 1662 - teksten [n] *texts*

De vertaalster moet nog vijf **teksten** vertalen.
The translator still has to translate another five **texts**.

### 1663 - respectievelijk [adj, adv] *respectively*

De broer en zus hebben **respectievelijk** vijf en drie albums uitgebracht.
The brother and sister have produced five and three albums, **respectively**.

### 1664 - vennootschap [n] *company*

Gefeliciteerd met jullie nieuwe **vennootschap**!
Congratulations on your new **company**!

### 1665 - mode [n] *fashion*

Teun draagt altijd de nieuwste **mode**.
Teun is always dressed in the latest **fashion**.

**1666 - groeide** [v] *to grow (singular subjects - past tense)*

Er **groeide** niets in de woestijn.
Nothing **grew** in the desert.

**1667 - verhogen** [v] *to raise (infinitive and plural subjects - present tense)*

De metro gaat de tarieven **verhogen**.
The metro is going to **raise** the fares.

**1668 - oudere** [adj] *older*

Woont je **oudere** zus ook in Leeuwarden?
Is your **older** sister also living in Leeuwarden?

**1669 - kende** [v] *to know (singular subjects - past tense)*

**Kende** je Lila al?
Did you already **know** Lila?

**1670 - concurrenten** [n] *competitors*

Onze **concurrenten** kunnen niet tegen deze reclamecampagne op!
Our **competitors** won't be able to beat this ad campaign!

**1671 - halve** [adj] *half*

Hier, voor ieder een **halve** peer.
Here, **half** a pear for each of you.

**1672 - kunstenaars** [n] *artists*

Niet alle **kunstenaars** hebben kunst gestudeerd.
Not all **artists** have studied art.

**1673 - instelling** [n] *configuration; institution; attitude*

Helpt deze **instelling** ook vluchtelingen?

Does this **institution** also help refugees?

### 1674 - goedkoop [adj] *cheap*

De tickets naar Aruba zijn nu heel **goedkoop**!
The tickets to Aruba are very **cheap** right now!

### 1675 - justitie [n] *judiciary; justice*

De minister van **Justitie** is afgetreden.
The Minister of **Justice** has stepped down.

### 1676 - gebieden [n, v] *areas; to ordain (infinitive and plural subjects - present tense)*

Welke **gebieden** in Zuid-Portugal raad je ons aan om te bezoeken?
Which **areas** in the south of Portugal do you recommend we visit?

### 1677 - g [n] *the letter G*

In het Nederlands kunnen de letters "ch" hetzelfde klinken als de **g**.
In Dutch, the letters "ch" can sound the same as the letter **G**.

### 1678 - fase [n] *phase*

De laatste **fase** van het project is begonnen.
The last **phase** of the project has started.

### 1679 - verboden [n, v] *prohibitions; to prohibit (plural subject - past tense; past participle)*

Roken is **verboden**.
Smoking is **prohibited**.

### 1680 - realiteit [n] *reality*

Fictie is het tegenovergestelde van **realiteit**.
Fiction is the opposite of **reality**.

### 1681 - wijnen [n] *wines*

De beste **wijnen** worden in de wijnwinkel verkocht.
The best **wines** are sold at the wine store.

### 1682 - vluchten [n, v] *flights; to flee (infinitive and plural subjects - present tense)*

Vanwege het slechte weer zijn er veel **vluchten** geannuleerd.
Due to the bad weather conditions, many **flights** were canceled.

### 1683 - r [n] *de letter R*

Ze vindt de Nederlandse **r** moeilijk om uit te spreken.
She thinks the letter **R** is difficult to pronounce in Dutch.

### 1684 - alternatief [adj, adv] *alternative(ly)*

Fred zag geen ander **alternatief** dan af te treden.
Fred didn't see any other **alternative** than to resign.

### 1685 - noorden [n] *north; northern*

In het **noorden** van Scandinavië zijn er veel rendieren.
In the **north** of Scandinavia, there are many reindeer.

### 1686 - vrede [n] *peace*

Droom jij ook van **vrede** op aarde?
Do you also dream about **peace** on Earth?

### 1687 - sommigen [pron] *some*

**Sommigen** werken liever 's ochtends, anderen liever 's avonds.
**Some** prefer working in the morning, others prefer working at night.

### 1688 - lening [n] *loan*

Het echtpaar gaat dit jaar hun **lening** aflossen.

The married couple is going to pay off their **loan** this year.

### 1689 - normen [n] *standards*

Onze grootouders hebben andere **normen** dan wij.
Our grandparents have different **standards** than us.

### 1690 - bescheiden [adj] *shy; modest*

Was de schrijver **bescheiden** of arrogant?
Was the writer **modest** or arrogant?

### 1691 - voorbeelden [n] *examples*

Deze zinnen zijn eenvoudige **voorbeelden** in het Nederlands.
These phrases are simple **examples** in Dutch.

### 1692 - sluit [v] *to close (singular subjects - present tense)*

De informatiebalie **sluit** om vijf uur.
The information desk **closes** at five o'clock.

### 1693 - medische [adj] *medical*

Haar **medische** kosten waren enorm hoog.
Her **medical** costs were enormous.

### 1694 - regionale [adj] *regional*

Er bestaan verrassend veel **regionale** dialecten in Nederland.
There are a surprising amount of **regional** dialects in The Netherlands.

### 1695 - deuren [n] *doors*

Alle **deuren** zitten op slot.
All the **doors** are locked.

### 1696 - culturele [adj] *cultural*

Er zijn veel **culturele** evenementen in Groningen.
There are a lot of **cultural** events in Groningen.

### 1697 - bescherming [n] *protection*

De getuige heeft **bescherming** nodig.
The witness needs **protection**.

### 1698 - begroting [n] *budget estimate*

De **begroting** is rond.
The **budget estimate** has been finished.

### 1699 - streek [n, v] *region; brushstroke; to smooth; to iron (singular subjects - past tense)*

In deze **streek** zijn veel dennenbomen.
In this **region** there are a lot of pine trees.

### 1700 - moeilijke [adj] *difficult*

Dat is een **moeilijke** vraag.
That's a **difficult** question.

### 1701 - koopt [v] *to buy (2ⁿᵈ and 3ʳᵈ person - present tense)*

De student **koopt** studieboeken online.
The student **buys** textbooks online.

### 1702 - wacht [n, v] *guard; to wait (singular subjects - present tense)*

**Wacht** op me!
**Wait** for me!

**1703 – risico's** [n] *risks*

De **risico's** van de operatie zijn klein.
The **risks** of the operation are small.

**1704 - planten** [n, v] *plants; to plant (infinitive and plural subjects - present tense)*

Je **planten** zijn enorm gegroeid!
Your **plants** have grown enormously!

**1705 - toepassingen** [n] *uses; applications*

Hij bestudeert **toepassingen** van UV-licht.
He studies UV-light **applications**.

**1706 - absolute** [adj] *absolute*

We kregen **absolute** creatieve vrijheid.
We were given **absolute** creative freedom.

**1707 - vervoer** [n, v] *transport; to transport (1ˢᵗ and 2ⁿᵈ person - present tense)*

Is het openbaar **vervoer** duur hier?
Is public **transport** expensive here?

**1708 - bestond** [v] *to exist (singular subjects - past tense)*

Het internet **bestond** in 1960 nog niet.
The Internet **didn't exist** yet in 1960.

**1709 - gekocht** [adj, v] *bought (past participle)*

Selma heeft vanochtend frambozen en aardbeien **gekocht**.
Selma has **bought** raspberries and strawberries this morning.

### 1710 - maatschappelijke [adj] *social, societal*

Deze instelling analyseert **maatschappelijke** problemen.
This institution analyzes **social** problems.

### 1711 - gewezen [v] *pointed (past participle)*

De politieman heeft ons de goede kant op **gewezen**.
The policeman has **pointed** us in the right direction.

### 1712 - plots [n, adj, adv] *plots; sudden(ly)*

Het ging **plots** regenen!
It **suddenly** started to rain!

### 1713 - waaraan [adv] *(of) what/which*

Jij hebt een badge **waaraan** mensen kunnen zien dat je
gehandicapt bent.
You have a badge **which** shows people that you're handicapped.

### 1714 - geest [n] *mind, spirit; ghost*

Het jongetje heeft een **geest** gezien!
The little boy has seen a **ghost**!

### 1715 - fondsen [n] *funds; trusts; foundations*

Lees hier het laatste nieuws over **fondsen**.
Read the latest news here about **funds**.

### 1716 - beperken [v] *to limit; to cut down (infinitive and plural subjects - present tense)*

Hoe gaan we de kosten **beperken**?
How are we going to **cut down** on costs?

### 1717 - overgenomen [v] *purchased; acquired; taken*

*over; copied (past participle)*

Ons bedrijf is **overgenomen** door een multinational.
Our company has been **purchased** by a multinational.

### 1718 - prestaties [n] *achievements*

De atleten hebben geweldige **prestaties** geleverd.
The athletes have delivered amazing **achievements**.

### 1719 - voorgesteld [v] *proposed; introduced (past participle)*

Ik heb eindelijk mijn **vriendin** aan mijn ouders voorgesteld!
I've finally **introduced** my girlfriend to my parents!

### 1720 - rijke [n, adj] *rich person; rich; copious*

Veel **rijke** mensen wonen in Bloemendaal.
Many **rich** people live in Bloemendaal.

### 1721 - militaire [adj] *military*

Veel Zuid-Amerikaanse landen hebben een **militaire** regering gehad.
Many South American countries have had a **military** government.

### 1722 - systemen [n] *systems*

Dit zijn de beste **systemen** om je financiën bij te houden.
These are the best **systems** to manage your finances.

### 1723 - kwart [n] *a quarter*

Bijna een **kwart** van de Belgen rookt.
Almost **a quarter** of Belgians smoke.

### 1724 - duidelijke [adj] *clear; obvious*

Bedankt voor uw **duidelijke** uitleg!
Thank you for your **clear** explanation!

### 1725 - luidt [v] *to ring; to sound; to say (2nd and 3rd person - present tense)*

De kerkklok **luidt** over tien minuten.
The church bell will **ring** in ten minutes.

### 1726 - toekomstige [adj] *future; prospective*

Welkom aan onze **toekomstige** parlementsleden!
Welcome to our **future** members of parliament.

### 1727 - leert [v] *to learn; to teach (2nd and 3rd person - present tense)*

De peuter **leert** alleen te eten.
The toddler **is learning** to eat by himself.

### 1728 - leeft [v] *to live (2nd and 3rd person - present tense)*

Onze schildpad **leeft** in de tuin.
Our turtle **lives** in the garden.

### 1729 - sprak [v] *to speak (singular subjects - past tense)*

De clown **sprak** met een gekke stem.
The clown **spoke** with a funny voice.

### 1730 - dorp [n] *village*

Het hele **dorp** werd versierd voor vijf mei.
The whole **village** was decorated for May fifth. *(May 5th is National Independence Day in The Netherlands, since the Second World War officially ended there on May 5, 1945)*

**1731 - zover** [conj, adv] *as far as; so far; ready*

We zijn **zover**!
We're **ready**!

**1732 - marktaandeel** [n] *market share*

Het **marktaandeel** van onze vennootschap groeit sterk.
The **market share** of our company is growing fast.

**1733 - motor** [n] *engine; motorbike*

De **motor** werkt prima.
The **engine** is working fine.

**1734 - velen** [n] *many*

**Velen** zakken voor hun eerste rijexamen.
**Many** fail their first driving exam.

**1735 - plaatselijke** [adj] *local*

De dokters besloten een **plaatselijke** verdoving te gebruiken.
The doctors decided to use **local** anesthesia.

**1736 - menselijke** [adj] *human(e)*

Hij studeert **menselijke** biologie.
He studies **human** biology.

**1737 - moord** [n, v] *murder; to kill (1$^{st}$ and 2$^{nd}$ person - present tense)*

De verdachte werd vrijgesproken van de **moord** op zijn vrouw.
The suspect was acquitted of his wife's **murder**.

**1738 - daalde** [v] *to decrease; to descend (singular*

*subjects - past tense)*

Haar lichaamstemperatuur **daalde** snel.
Her body temperature **was decreasing** quickly.

### 1739 - afspraken [n] *appointments; agreements*

We moeten al onze **afspraken** afzeggen.
We have to cancel all of our **appointments**.

### 1740 - vreemd [adj, adv] *strange(ly)*

Wat **vreemd**, mijn sleutels zijn opeens verdwenen.
That's **strange**, my keys have suddenly disappeared.

### 1741 - speelde [v] *to play (an instrument) (singular subjects - past tense)*

De familie **speelde** altijd bordspellen op zondag.
The family always **played** board games on Sundays.

### 1742 - professor [n] *professor*

De **professor** was nergens te vinden!
The **professor** was nowhere to be found!

### 1743 - duurt [v] *to last; to take (time) ($2^{nd}$ and $3^{rd}$ person - present tense)*

Deze lezing **duurt** drie uur.
This lecture **lasts** three hours.

### 1744 - min [n, adv] *minus; minus sign*

Acht **min** vijf is drie.
Eight **minus** five is three.

### 1745 - gedelegeerd [v] *delegated (past participle)*

De baas heeft een aantal taken aan mij **gedelegeerd**.

The boss has **delegated** a number of tasks to me.

### 1746 - graden [n] *degrees; ranks*

Het is twintig **graden**.
It's twenty **degrees**.

### 1747 - evenmin [adv] *neither; nor*

Zij houdt niet van melk, ik **evenmin**.
She doesn't like milk, **neither** do I.

### 1748 - tenslotte [adv] *after all*

Nog meer taart voor jou, het is **tenslotte** je verjaardag!
More cake for you, it's your birthday **after all**!

### 1749 - vlucht [n, v] *flight; to flee (singular subjects - present tense)*

Een prettige **vlucht** gewenst!
We wish you a nice **flight!**

### 1750 - leidde [v] *to lead (to) (singular subjects - past tense)*

De manager **leidde** zijn team heel goed.
The manager **led** his team very well.

### 1751 - bus [n] *tin; bus*

Dit is de verkeerde **bus**!
This is the wrong **bus**!

### 1752 - ontstaat [v] *to originate; to emerge (2nd and 3rd person - present tense)*

Weet je hoe een tsunami **ontstaat**?
Do you know how a tsunami **emerges**?

### 1753 - onvoldoende [n, adj] *failing grade; insufficient*

Er is **onvoldoende** koffie voor alle aanwezigen.

There's **insufficient** coffee for everyone present.

### 1754 - lichte [adj] *light*

Het model at meestal een **lichte** avondmaaltijd.

The model usually ate a **light** dinner.

### 1755 - hopen [n, v] *heaps; to hope (infinitive and plural subjects - present tense)*

We **hopen** dat de zon morgen schijnt!

We **hope** the sun will shine tomorrow!

### 1756 - tenminste [adv] *on the condition that; at least*

We gaan **tenminste** voorlopig niet verhuizen.

**At least** for the time being, we won't move.

### 1757 - kranten [n] *newspapers*

Die oude **kranten** kunnen weg.

Those old **newspapers** can be thrown out.

### 1758 - verschenen [v] *to appear (plural subjects - past tense; past participle)*

Er **verschenen** opeens rare vlekken op mijn armen.

Strange blotches suddenly **appeared** on my arms.

### 1759 - theater [n] *theater*

Dit **theater** heeft geen parkeerplaats.

This **theater** doesn't have a parking lot.

**1760 - welk** [pron] *which*

Welk boek heb je al gelezen?
Which book have you already read?

**1761 - twijfel** [n, v] *doubt; to doubt (1ˢᵗ and 2ⁿᵈ person - present tense)*

Ik twijfel soms te veel aan mezelf.
I doubt myself too much sometimes.

**1762 - moeilijker** [adj, adv] *more difficult*

Het videospel werd steeds moeilijker.
The video game got more and more difficult.

**1763 - ernstig** [adj, adv] *serious(ly), severe(ly)*

De verwondingen waren niet ernstig.
The injuries weren't severe.

**1764 - gebleven** [v] *stayed (past participle)*

Haar neven waren tot één uur 's nachts gebleven.
Her cousins had stayed until one o'clock in the morning.

**1765 - gespecialiseerd** [v] *specialized (past participle)*

Dokter Laan heeft zich gespecialiseerd in tropenziekten.
Doctor Laan has specialized in tropical diseases.

**1766 - wetenschappelijke** [adj] *scientific*

Mijn opa leest graag over wetenschappelijke doorbraken.
My grandfather likes reading about scientific breakthroughs.

**1767 - ofwel** [conj] *either ... or*

Ofwel we gaan allemaal, ofwel niemand gaat!

**Either** everyone goes, **or** nobody goes!

### 1768 - standpunt [n] *point of view*

Vanuit zijn **standpunt** was er geen enkele twijfel.
From his **point of view**, there was no doubt at all.

### 1769 - ontslag [n] *dismissal or resignation from employment*

Mijn assistente heeft opeens haar **ontslag** ingediend.
My assistant has suddenly presented her **resignation**.

### 1770 - zaten [v] *to sit (plural subjects - past tense)*

In het park **zaten** veel mensen.
A lot of people were **sitting** in the park.

### 1771 - zwakke [adj] *weak*

De **zwakke** benen van het oude paard hielden het niet vol.
The old horse's **weak** legs couldn't keep going.

### 1772 - kansen [n] *chances; opportunities*

Wat zijn onze **kansen**?
What are our **chances**?

### 1773 - studies [n] *course; research studies*

Universiteit Leiden biedt veel interessante **studies** aan.
Leiden University offers many interesting **courses**.

### 1774 - programma's [n] *programs*

Er staan te veel **programma's** op jouw computer.
There are too many **programs** on your computer.

### 1775 - verkeer [n] *traffic; to be in a certain*

*location/state (1<sup>st</sup> and 2<sup>nd</sup> person - present tense)*

Er was gisteren weinig **verkeer**.
There was not much **traffic** yesterday.

### 1776 - huwelijk [n] *marriage*

Ons **huwelijk** gaat niet goed.
Our **marriage** isn't going well.

### 1777 - kwaad [n, adj. adv] *evil; angry*

Ze brak een bord en haar vader werd **kwaad**.
She broke a plate and her father got **angry**.

### 1778 - koper [n] *copper; buyer*

De makelaar heeft een **koper** voor hun huis!
The realtor has a **buyer** for their house!

### 1779 - eiland [n] *island*

Ameland is een prachtig **eiland** ten noorden van Friesland.
Ameland is a beautiful **island** north of Friesland.

### 1780 - democratie [n] *democracy*

Een dictatuur is het tegenovergestelde van een **democratie**.
A dictatorship is the opposite of a **democracy**.

### 1781 - ziekenhuis [n] *hospital*

De zwangere vrouw nam een taxi naar het **ziekenhuis**.
The pregnant woman took a taxi to the **hospital**.

### 1782 - gedeeltelijk [adj, adv] *partial(ly)*

De kerk is gisteren **gedeeltelijk** ingestort.
The church **partially** collapsed yesterday.

### 1783 - wit [n, adj, adv] *white*

Het uniform is een **wit** t-shirt met een zwarte broek.
The uniform is a **white** t-shirt with black pants.

### 1784 - miljoenen [n] *millions*

Onze hersenen hebben vele **miljoenen** neuronale connecties.
Our brains have many **millions** of neural connections.

### 1785 - slachtoffer [n] *casualty; victim*

Het verkeersongeluk heeft één **slachtoffer** veroorzaakt.
The traffic accident has caused one **casualty**.

### 1786 - producent [n] *manufacturer; producer*

De **producent** zocht een extra assistent.
The **producer** was looking for an extra assistant.

### 1787 - kleren [n] *clothes*

Je geeft te veel uit aan **kleren**!
You spend too much on **clothes**!

### 1788 - hoek [n] *angle; corner*

Zet je de bezem in de **hoek**?
Will you put the broom in the **corner**?

### 1789 - dans [n, v] *dance; to dance (1$^{st}$ and 2$^{nd}$ person - present tense)*

Deze **dans** is te ingewikkeld voor kinderen.
This **dance** is too complicated for children.

### 1790 - kust [n] *coast; to kiss (2$^{nd}$ and 3$^{rd}$ person - present tense)*

Er liggen mooie duinen aan de Nederlandse **kust**.

There are nice dunes on the Dutch **coast**.

## 1791 - voornamelijk [adv] *mainly*

Ons restaurant verkoopt **voornamelijk** friet en frikandellen.
Our restaurant **mainly** sells French fries and *frikandel. (traditional Dutch sausage)*

## 1792 - directie [n] *management; board*

Meneer Mol is de secretaris van de **directie**.
Mister Mol is secretary of the **board**.

## 1793 - bedrijfsleven [n] *business world*

Veel contacten hebben is uiterst belangrijk in het **bedrijfsleven**.
Having many contacts is extremely important in the **business world**.

## 1794 - normale [adj] *normal*

Ze hebben **normale** en veganistische pannenkoeken.
They have **normal** and vegan pancakes.

## 1795 - produceren [v] *to produce (plural subjects - present tense)*

Die fabrieken **produceren** cement.
Those factories **produce** cement.

## 1796 - snelheid [n] *speed*

Deze auto bereikt zijn hoogste **snelheid** binnen twee minuten.
This car reaches its top **speed** within two minutes.

## 1797 - besloot [v] *to decide (singular subjects - past tense)*

De jongen **besloot** dat hij dierenarts wilde worden.

The boy **decided** he wanted to become a vet.

### 1798 - selectie [n] *selection; compilation*

We e-mailen je de lijst met onze **selectie**.
We'll email you the list with our **selection**.

### 1799 - oppositie [n] *opposition*

Wat vindt de **oppositie** van uw voorstel?
What does the **opposition** think about your proposal?

### 1800 - ronde [n, adj] *round*

Dit is de laatste **ronde**!
This is the last **round**!

### 1801 - dikwijls [adv] *often*

De studenten gingen **dikwijls** studeren in de bibliotheek.
The students would **often** study at the library.

### 1802 - looptijd [n] *term; duration*

De **looptijd** van onze woonverzekering is één jaar.
The **term** of our home insurance is one year.

### 1803 - anderzijds [adv] *on the other hand*

Enerzijds hield ze van haar nieuwe baan, **anderzijds** miste ze het freelancen.
On the one hand, she liked her new job, **on the other hand**, she missed freelancing.

### 1804 - bleven [v] *to stay; to continue (plural subjects - past tense)*

De vogels **bleven** naar het vogelhuis komen.

The birds **continued** to come to the bird house.

### 1805 - bodem [n] *ground; bottom*

De Titanic ligt op de **bodem** van de zee.
The Titanic is lying at the **bottom** of the sea.

### 1806 - ambtenaren [n] *civil servants*

Alle **ambtenaren** krijgen volgende week een extra dag vrij.
All **civil servants** will get an extra day off next week.

### 1807 - kantoren [n] *offices*

Drie **kantoren** in Rotterdam zijn gisteren in rook opgegaan.
Three **offices** in Rotterdam have gone up in smoke yesterday.

### 1808 - wetenschap [n] *knowledge; science*

De **wetenschap** kan sommige verschijnselen niet verklaren.
**Science** can't explain certain phenomena.

### 1809 - veroorzaakt [v] *to cause (2nd and 3rd person - present tense; past participle)*

De brand was door een kortsluiting **veroorzaakt**.
The fire was **caused** by a short circuit.

### 1810 - uitgaven [n] *expenses*

We willen onze huishoudelijke **uitgaven** verminderen.
We want to reduce our household **expenses**.

### 1811 - beschikking [n] *disposal; regulation; ordinance*

Ik sta tot uw **beschikking**, mevrouw.
I am at your **disposal**, ma'am.

### 1812 - gebruikers [n] *users*

De helpdesk helpt **gebruikers** met vragen.
The help desk helps users with **questions**.

### 1813 - rand [n] *edge; outskirts*

De dierentuin zit aan de **rand** van de stad.
The zoo is located on the **outskirts** of the city.

### 1814 - gedeelte [n] *part*

Het laatste **gedeelte** van de film is heel eng.
The last **part** of the movie is very scary.

### 1815 - verandert [n] *to change (2nd and 3rd person - present tense)*

Jij **verandert** nooit!
You never **change**!

### 1816 - fenomeen [n] *phenomenon*

Populisme is een ingewikkeld **fenomeen**.
Populism is a complicated **phenomenon**.

### 1817 - interesse [n] *interest*

Ze hadden geen **interesse** in de aanbieding.
They didn't have any **interest** in the special offer.

### 1818 - stoffen [n, v] *substances; fabric; subject matter; to dust (infinitive and plural subjects - present tense)*

We moeten die planken weer **stoffen**.
We have to **dust** off those shelves again!

### 1819 - bevindt [v] *to be located; to find oneself (2nd and*

*3rd person - present tense)*

Het stadhuis **bevindt** zich op het centrale plein.
The city hall **is located** on the main square.

### 1820 - voorwaarde [n] *condition*

We tekenen, onder één **voorwaarde**.
We'll sign, under one **condition**.

### 1821 - groen [n, adj, adv] *green*

**Groen** vond ze een rustgevende kleur.
She thought **green** was a calming color.

### 1822 - beleggen [v] *to make a sandwich; to invest (infinitive and plural subjects - present tense)*

Hij overweegt in vastgoed te **beleggen**.
He is considering **investing** in real estate.

### 1823 - vrouwelijke [adj] *female; feminine*

De sportschool heeft eindelijk zijn eerste **vrouwelijke** manager.
The gym, finally, has its first **female** manager.

### 1824 - aparte [adj] *separate; unusual*

Wat een **aparte** hoed heeft die zanger op!
What an **unusual** hat is that singerwearing!

### 1825 - verschijnen [v] *to appear; to come out (infinitive and plural subjects - present tense)*

We zagen langzaam de volle maan **verschijnen**.
We saw the full moon **come out** slowly.

### 1826 - zagen [n] *to see (plural subjects - past tense); to*

*saw (plural subjects - present tense)*

**Zagen** julllie die vallende ster?
Did you **see** that falling star?

### 1827 - brede [adj] *broad, wide*

De sollicitant had een **brede** kennis van projectmanagement.
The applicant had **broad** project management knowledge.

### 1828 - monetaire [adj] *monetary*

Veranderingen in ons **monetaire** beleid zijn nodig.
Changes to our **monetary** policy are necessary.

### 1829 - realiseren [v] *to realize (infinitive and plural subjects - present tense)*

Ze moet zich **realiseren** dat ze een ernstig probleem heeft.
She has **to realize** that she's got a serious problem.

### 1830 - sterker [adj, adv] *stronger; sturdier*

Deze cocktail is **sterker** dan de vorige!
This cocktail is **stronger** than the last one!

### 1831 - ploeg [n, v] *team; plow; to plow (1$^{st}$ and 2$^{nd}$ person - present tense)*

Welke **ploeg** gaat winnen, denk je?
What **team** do you think will win?

### 1832 - elf [num] *eleven*

Iedere ploeg heeft **elf** voetbalspelers op het veld.
Each team has **eleven** soccer players on the field.

### 1833 - werklozen [n] *unemployed people*

Het aantal **werklozen** is weer gestegen.

The amount of **unemployed people** has risen again.

### 1834 - feiten [n] *facts*

Hier zijn de harde **feiten**.
Here are the hard **facts**.

### 1835 - duren [v] *to last; to take (time) (infinitive and plural subjects - present tense)*

Het project gaat iets langer **duren**.
The project will **take** a little longer.

### 1836 - stof [n] *substance; fabric; subject matter; to dust (1st and 2nd person - present tense)*

Het examen zal over deze **stof** gaan.
The exam will be about this **subject matter**.

### 1837 - uitstekend [adj, adv] *excellent*

Na de massage voelde Tim zich **uitstekend**!
After the massage, Tim felt **excellent**!

### 1838 - geluk [n] *luck; happiness*

Jij hebt **geluk** gehad!
You've had good **luck**!

### 1839 - ruime [adj] *spacious*

We willen een auto met een ruime **achterbak**.
We want a car with a spacious **trunk**.

### 1840 - vergelijken [v] *to compare (infinitive and plural subjects - present tense)*

Niet appels met peren **vergelijken**!
Don't **compare** apples and pears!

### 1841 - woningen [n] *houses*

Alle buren versierden hun **woningen** voor het feest.
All the neighbors decorated their **houses** for the party.

### 1842 - volop [adv] *fully; in abundance*

Er was **volop** eten op de verjaardag!
There was food **in abundance** at the birthday!

### 1843 - jongen [n] *boy; young animals; to bear young (infinitive and plural subjects - present tense)*

Er is een nieuwe **jongen** in onze klas.
There's a new **boy** in our class.

### 1844 - regel [n] *rule; line (in a text); to arrange (1$^{st}$ and 2$^{nd}$ person - present tense)*

Wat betekent de derde **regel** van het gedicht?
What does the third **line** in the poem mean?

### 1845 - qua [adv] *in terms of*

**Qua** persoonlijkheid is Wilhelm perfect voor de baan.
**In terms of** personality, Wilhelm is perfect for the job.

### 1846 - hout [n] *wood*

Hun tuinbank is gemaakt van mooi **hout**.
Their garden bench is made of beautiful **wood**.

### 1847 - negatief [adj, adv] *negative(ly)*

De zwangerschapstest was **negatief**.
The pregnancy test was **negative**.

### 1848 - vooral [adv] *especially*

Mijn schoonzus houdt van sporten, **vooral** van hardlopen.

My sister-in-law likes sports, **especially** running.

### 1849 - richt [v] *to aim; to focus on (singular subjects - present tense)*

De voetbalspeler **richt** niet goed en mist het goal.

The soccer player doesn't **aim** well and misses the goal.

### 1850 - drukken [n, v] *pressures; editions; to push (a button); to print (infinitive and plural subjects - present tense)*

Nu op de enter-knop **drukken**.

Now **press** the enter-button.

### 1851 - stil [adj. adv] *quiet(ly), calm(ly)*

Het is heerlijk **stil** hier op de heide.

It's wonderfully **quiet** here on the moor.

### 1852 - concrete [adj] *concrete; tangible*

Deze partij heeft geen **concrete** plannen om werkloosheid aan te pakken.

This party doesn't have any **concrete** plans to tackle unemployment.

### 1853 - belangrijker [adj] *more important*

De vrouw vond eerlijkheid **belangrijker** dan uiterlijk.

The woman thought honesty was **more important** than looks.

### 1854 - warm [adj, adv] *warm(ly)*

Bij **warm** weer groeit deze plant sneller.

In **warm** weather, this plant grows faster.

### 1855 - afval [n] *waste*

Dit **afval** moet in de vuilnisbak.
This **waste** has to go in the trash can.

### 1856 - muur [n] *wall*

Die **muur** heeft hele mooie graffiti.
That **wall** has very nice graffiti.

### 1857 - minst [n, adj] *least*

Wie het **minst** lacht, wint de wedstrijd!
The one who **laughs** the least, wins the competition!

### 1858 - lieten [v] *to let (plural subjects - past tense)*

De pinguïns **lieten** hun vissen niet los.
The penguins didn't **let** go of their fish.

### 1859 - vertrekken [n, v] *rooms; to leave (infinitive and plural subjects - present tense)*

Jongens, we moeten **vertrekken**!
Guys, we have to **leave**!

### 1860 - veeleer [adv] *rather, preferably*

Dat is geen reiger, het is **veeleer** een soort kraanvogel.
That's not a heron, but **rather** a kind of crane.

### 1861 - regeling [n] *regulation; arrangement*

Kunnen we een **regeling** treffen over de kinderen?
Can we make an **arrangement** concerning the children?

### 1862 - zaal [n] *auditorium, hall*

Is deze **zaal** groot genoeg voor het feest?

Is this **auditorium** big enough for the party?

### 1863 - literatuur [n] *literature*

Qua **literatuur** hield ze het meest van poëzie.
In terms of **literature**, she liked poetry most.

### 1864 - slaat [n] *to hit (2nd and 3rd person - present tense)*

Een drummer **slaat** op het drumstel.
A drummer **hits** the drum kit.

### 1865 - trein [n] *train*

Ze neemt dagelijks de **trein**.
She takes the **train** every day.

### 1866 - zulke [pron] *such; those kinds of*

Het spijt me, **zulke** pruiken hebben we niet.
I'm sorry, we don't have **those kinds of** wigs.

### 1867 - geopend [adj, v] *opened (past participle)*

De nieuwe snoepwinkel is gisteren **geopend**.
The new candy store **opened** yesterday.

### 1868 - tijdje [n] *a while*

We wachten al een **tijdje**.
We've been waiting for **a while**.

### 1869 - luchthaven [n] *airport*

Schiphol is de grootste **luchthaven** van Nederland.
Schiphol is the biggest **airport** in The Netherlands.

### 1870 - administratie [n] *administration, management*

De **administratie** heeft haar definitieve beslissing nog niet genomen.

**Administration** hasn't taken their final decision yet.

### 1871 - voeten [n] *feet*

Je **voeten** zijn niet even groot!

Your **feet** aren't the same size!

### 1872 - voedsel [n] *food*

Te veel **voedsel** wordt verspild.

Too much **food** is being wasted.

### 1873 - erbij [adv] *with it*

Krijgen ze brood **erbij**?

Are they getting bread **with it**?

### 1874 - destijds [adv] *at that time, then*

**Destijds** woonden we in Scheveningen.

We lived in Scheveningen **then**.

### 1875 - sporen [n] *spores; traces; (rail) tracks*

De jager vond **sporen** van een hertenfamilie.

The hunter found **tracks** belonging to a deer family.

### 1876 - evenwicht [n] *balance*

Capoeira spelen helpt je met je **evenwicht**!

Playing capoeira helps you with your **balance**!

### 1877 - architectuur [n] *architecture*

Hij is een boek aan het lezen over klassieke **architectuur**.

He's reading a book about classical **architecture**.

### 1878 - munten [n] *coins; to mint (infinitive and plural subjects - present tense)*

Buitenlandse **munten** verzamelen is leuk.
Collecting foreign **coins** is fun.

### 1879 - troepen [n] *troops*

De **troepen** komen eraan!
The **troops** are coming!

### 1880 - wél [n, interj, adv] *well; as an adverb it's used to contradict a previous negative statement*

Hij had geen tijd? Dat had hij **wél**!
He didn't have time? Yes, he **did**!

### 1881 - onderdelen [n] *parts*

We hebben de extra **onderdelen** besteld.
We've ordered the extra **parts**.

### 1882 - nieuwste [adj] *newest; latest*

Jaap heeft altijd de **nieuwste** mobiel.
Jaap always has the **latest** cell phone.

### 1883 - poging [n] *attempt*

Oké, nog één **poging** dan.
Okay, one more **attempt** then.

### 1884 - ouder [n, adj] *parent; older*

Je ziet er geen dag **ouder** uit!
You don't look a day **older**!

### 1885 - nergens [adv] *nowhere, not ... anywhere*

Ze hebben **nergens** luiers.

They do **not** have diapers **anywhere**.

### 1886 - machines [n] *machines*

Kunnen **machines** jouw baan doen?

Can **machines** do your job?

### 1887 - as [n] *axis; axle*

De aarde draait om haar **as**.

The Earth spins on its **axis**.

### 1888 - relaties [n] *relations, relationships*

Mijn **relaties** lopen altijd na een jaar stuk.

My **relationships** always break down after a year.

### 1889 - wagens [n] *wagons; cars*

Die **wagens** zijn rijp voor de sloop!

Those **cars** are ready to be demolished!

### 1890 - blik [n] *tin; look*

Wat betekent die **blik**?

What does that **look** mean?

### 1891 - particuliere [adj] *private*

We kunnen die **particuliere** school niet betalen.

We can't afford that **private** school.

### 1892 - duurder [adj] *more expensive*

De treinkaartjes zijn **duurder** tijdens het spitsuur.

Train tickets are **more expensive** during rush hour.

### 1893 - conflict [n] *conflict; disagreement*

Hij had een moeilijk innerlijk **conflict**.
He had a difficult internal **conflict**.

### 1894 - reputatie [n] *reputation*

Heeft Universiteit Maastricht een goede **reputatie**?
Does Maastricht University have a good **reputation**?

### 1895 - hou [v] *to hold; to keep; to love (1st and 2nd person - present tense)*

**Hou** die boeken maar!
Just **keep** those books!

### 1896 - uitstekende [adj] *excellent*

Deze sollicitant heeft **uitstekende** ervaring.
This applicant has **excellent** experience.

### 1897 - vak [n] *profession; section; (school) subject*

Scheikunde was haar favoriete **vak** op school.
Chemistry was her favorite **subject** at school.

### 1898 - waarheid [n] *truth*

Dat klinkt niet als de **waarheid**.
That doesn't sound like the **truth**.

### 1899 - zorgde [v] *to take care of; to look after (singular subjects - past tense)*

Mijn schoonzus **zorgde** voor de huisdieren tijdens onze vakantie.
My sister-in-law **looked after** the pets during our vacation.

### 1900 - categorie [n] *category*

De eerste **categorie** is: bekende mensen.

The first **category** is: famous people.

### 1901 - spoor [n] *spore; trace; (rail) track*

Er loopt een kat over het **spoor**!

There's a cat walking on the **rail track**!

### 1902 - ontwikkelingen [n] *developments*

Er zijn geen nieuwe **ontwikkelingen**.

There aren't any new **developments**.

### 1903 - langere [adj] *longer*

Verkopen jullie ook **langere** gordijnen?

Do you also sell **longer** curtains?

### 1904 - advocaat [n] *lawyer, attorney; Dutch egg brandy*

Luister naar hem, hij is je **advocaat**!

Listen to him, he's your **lawyer**!

### 1905 - premie [n] *premium; bonus*

De **premie** van mijn verzekering is nu veel te duur.

My insurance **premium** is now much too expensive.

### 1906 - lijnen [n, v] *(telephone) lines; plot; to diet (infinitive and plural subjects - present tense)*

The schilder Mondriaan gebruikte alleen rechte **lijnen**.

The painter Mondriaan only used straight **lines**.

### 1907 - koos [v] *to choose (singular subjects - past tense)*

De jury **koos** de winnaar.

The jury **chose** the winner.

### 1908 - geleverd [v] *delivered (past participle)*

Uw bestelling is zojuist **geleverd**.
Your order has just been **delivered**.

### 1909 - mond [n] *mouth*

Niet met je **mond** vol praten, zei de moeder.
Don't talk with your **mouth** full, said the mother.

### 1910 - veranderingen [n] *changes*

Mijn grootouders willen geen **veranderingen**.
My grandparents don't want any **changes**.

### 1911 - kleiner [adj, adv] *smaller*

Ze wilde een **kleiner** stukje cake.
She wanted a **smaller** piece of cake.

### 1912 - slotte [n] *almost exclusively used in the expression "ten slotte", meaning finally*

Ik heb ten **slotte** de knoop doorgehakt.
I have **finally** made the decision.

### 1913 - jarenlang [adv] *for years*

Ze gaan al **jarenlang** naar dezelfde camping.
They've been going to the same camping ground **for years**.

### 1914 - schilderijen [n] *paintings*

Deze **schilderijen** moeten daar opgehangen worden.
These **paintings** have to be mounted over there.

### 1915 - schip [n] *ship*

De containers worden op het **schip** geladen.
The containers will be stowed onto the **ship**.

### 1916 - schaal [n] *scale; dish; shell*

Deze **schaal** is voor de hapjes.
This **dish** is for the snacks.

### 1917 - materialen [n] *materials*

De kosten van de **materialen** zijn gestegen.
The costs of the **materials** have risen.

### 1918 - gedragen [v] *to behave (infinitive and plural subjects - present tense; past participle); carried (past participle)*

Hoe **gedragen** jouw leerlingen zich?
How do your students **behave**?

### 1919 - grondig [adj, adv] *thorough(ly)*

De school werd **grondig** schoongemaakt.
The school was cleaned **thoroughly**.

### 1920 - directe [adj] *direct*

Dit is de **directe** trein naar Berlijn.
This is the **direct** train to Berlin.

### 1921 - wapens [n] *weapons*

Ze hebben prehistorische **wapens** in het bos gevonden!
They've found prehistoric **weapons** in the woods!

### 1922 - geconfronteerd [v] *confronted (past participle)*

De politici werden **geconfronteerd** met de demonstranten.
The politicians were **confronted** by the protesters.

### 1923 - woordvoerder [n] *spokesman*

De **woordvoerder** van de gemeente gaf een verklaring.
The **spokesman** of the municipality gave a statement.

### 1924 - oorzaak [n] *cause*

De **oorzaak** van de brand was niet bekend.
The **cause** of the fire wasn't known.

### 1925 - toestel [n] *device; aircraft*

Het **toestel** maakte een noodlanding.
The **aircraft** made an emergency landing.

### 1926 - stilaan [adv] *gradually; unnoticed*

Ze wordt **stilaan** een jonge vrouw.
She's **gradually** becoming a young woman.

### 1927 - wetenschappelijk [adj, adv] *scientifical(ly)*

Die hypothese is nog niet **wetenschappelijk** bewezen.
That hypothesis hasn't been proven **scientifically**.

### 1928 - woont [v] *to live (2$^{nd}$ and 3$^{rd}$ person - present tense)*

Sanne **woont** niet meer naast ons.
Sanne no longer **lives** next to us.

### 1929 - investeerders [n] *investors*

De **investeerders** eisen resultaten!

The **investors** are demanding results!

### 1930 - tekenen [n, v] *signs; to draw (infinitive and plural subjects - present tense)*

Zullen we het landschap **tekenen**?
Shall we **draw** the landscape?

### 1931 - boeren [n, v] *farmers; to burp (infinitive and plural subjects - present tense)*

Morgen gaan de **boeren** de groentes oogsten.
The **farmers** will harvest the vegetables tomorrow.

### 1932 - serie [n] *series*

Dit is het eerste boek van de **serie**.
This is the first book of the **series**.

### 1933 - nadien [adv] *afterwards*

**Nadien** is hij afgevaren.
He set sail **afterwards**.

### 1934 - werkelijk [adj, adv] *true; truly*

Het uitzicht is **werkelijk** schitterend.
The view is **truly** magnificent.

### 1935 - opgebouwd [adj, v] *built; developed; composed of (past participle)*

We hebben na jaren een goede relatie **opgebouwd**.
After years, we have **built** a good relationship.

### 1936 - bijdragen [v] *to contribute (infinitive and plural subjects - present tense)*

Mijn kinderen willen graag ook wat **bijdragen**.

My children would also like to **contribrute** with something.

### 1937 - hoeven [n, v] *hooves; to have to; to want (infinitive and plural subjects - present tense)*

Wij **hoeven** niets meer te drinken.
We don't **want** anything else to drink.

### 1938 - gekoppeld [adj, v] *linked; coupled (past participle)*

De Belgische school is **gekoppeld** aan een Poolse school.
The Belgian school is **linked** to a Polish school.

### 1939 - vrees [n, v] *fear; to be afraid (1$^{st}$ and 2$^{nd}$ person - present tense)*

Ik **vrees** dat mevr. Groot er vandaag niet is.
**I'm afraid** Mrs. Groot isn't in today.

### 1940 - haven [n] *port*

De **haven** van Rotterdam is grootste **haven** van Europa.
The **Port** of Rotterdam is the biggest **port** in Europe.

### 1941 - dagelijkse [adj] *daily*

De bejaarde man had een vaste **dagelijkse** routine.
The elderly man had a fixed **daily** routine.

### 1942 - leiders [n] *leaders*

Zelfs de **leiders** wisten niet wat ze moesten doen!
Even the **leaders** didn't know what to do!

### 1943 - slagen [n, v] *strikes; to succeed; to pass an exam (infinitive and plural subjects - present tense)*

Alle leerlingen willen natuurlijk **slagen** voor het examen.

Of course, all students want to **pass the exam.**

### 1944 - ontworpen [adj, v] *designed (past participle)*

Het Kröller-Müller Museum werd **ontworpen** door de Belgische architect Henry van de Velde.
The Kröller-Müller Museum was **designed** by Belgian architect Henry van de Velde.

### 1945 - aard [n] *nature; character; type*

Dat zit niet in mijn **aard**.
That's not in my **nature**.

### 1946 - exemplaren [n] *examples; copies; specimens*

We hebben drie prachtige **exemplaren** van de ratelslang gezien.
We saw three beautiful **specimens** of the rattlesnake.

### 1947 - breed [adj, adv] *broad(ly), wide(ly)*

De huiskamer is zes meter **breed**.
The living room is six meters **wide**.

### 1948 - vooruit [adv, interj] *forward; beforehand; come on!*

**Vooruit**, we moeten vertrekken!
**Come on**, we have to leave!

### 1949 - ermee [adv] *with it/that*

Hier is het examen, veel succes **ermee**!
Here's the exam, good luck **with it**!

### 1950 - pak [n, v] *box; suit; to catch; to get; to pack; to*

*dupe (1ˢᵗ and 2ⁿᵈ person - present tense)*

Mooi **pak**, Tom!
Nice **suit**, Tom!

### 1951 - burger [n] *citizen; civilian; hamburger*

Voor mij graag mosterd op de **burger**!
Mustard on the **burger** for me, please!

### 1952 - uitgegeven [v] *published; spent (past participle)*

We hebben te veel **uitgegeven** tijdens de vakantie.
We've **spent** too much during our vacation.

### 1953 - treden [n, v] *steps; to step*

De torentrap had zeventig **treden**.
The stairs of the tower had seventy **steps**.

### 1954 - bekeken [v] *watched; scrutinized (past participle)*

De paspoorten worden nauwkeurig **bekeken**.
The passports are **examined** with scrutiny.

### 1955 - alweer [adv] *again*

Eten we **alweer** gekookte aardappelen?
Are we eating boiled potatoes **again**?

### 1956 - stukje [n] *bit; little piece*

Het is een nog een kleine **stukje** verder.
It's just a little **bit** further.

### 1957 - muren [n] *walls*

Er zijn scheuren in de **muren** gekomen door de aardbeving.
Cracks have appeared in the **walls** because of the earthquake.

277

### 1958 - typisch [adj, adv] *typical(ly)*

Een boterham met hagelslag is een **typisch** Nederlands ontbijt.
A chocolate sprinkle sandwich is a **typical** Dutch breakfast.

### 1959 - arbeiders [n] *laborers, workers*

De **arbeiders** stichtten een vakbond.
The **laborers** founded a union.

### 1960 - oorspronkelijke [adj] *original, indigenous*

De **oorspronkelijke** bewoners van Australië zijn de Aboriginals.
The **indigenous** inhabitants of Australia are the Aboriginals.

### 1961 - aanbieden [v] *to offer; to sell (infinitive and plural subjects - present tense)*

Kan ik u verder nog iets **aanbieden**?
Can I **offer** you anything else?

### 1962 - kleding [n] *clothing*

Hier verkopen ze tweedehands **kleding**.
They sell second-hand **clothing** here.

### 1963 - lagen [n, v] *layers; to lie (plural subjects - past tense)*

De handdoeken **lagen** alweer op de grond!
The towels **were lying** on the floor again!

### 1964 - rechts [adj. adv] *(on the) right; right-handed; right wing*

Het station is hier **rechts**.
The station is on the **right** here.

### 1965 - verbetering [n] *improvement*

Ik zie een hele **verbetering** in je woordenschat!
I can see a lot of **improvement** in your vocabulary!

### 1966 - lezer [n] *reader*

De doorsnee **lezer** van ons blad zoekt advies over mode.
The average **reader** of our magazine is looking for advice about fashion.

### 1967 - hotels [n] *hotels*

Dit is één van de slechtste **hotels** waar ik ooit heb overnacht.
This is one of the worst **hotels** I've ever stayed at.

### 1968 - Belg [n] *Belgian person*

Een **Belg** kan vaak twee talen spreken.
A **Belgian person** often speaks two languages.

### 1969 - durven [v] *to dare (infinitive and plural subjects - present tense)*

De kinderen **durven** niet van de glijbaan af.
The children don't **dare** to go down the slide.

### 1970 - participatie [n] *participation*

Uw **participatie** wordt erg op prijs gesteld.
Your **participation** is highly appreciated.

### 1971 - technisch [adj, adv] *technical(ly)*

We hebben een enorm **technisch** probleem.
We are having an enormous **technical** problem.

### 1972 - verspreid [adj, v] *spread (past participle)*

Het slechte nieuws was snel **verspreid**.
The bad news was **spread** quickly.

### 1973 - respect [n] *respect*

Meneer de Vries toonde niemand **respect**.
Mister de Vries didn't show **respect** to anyone.

### 1974 - originele [adj] *original*

Het **originele** script is veel veranderd.
The **original** script has changed a lot.

### 1975 - beroemde [adj] *famous*

Anouk is een **beroemde** Nederlandse zangeres.
Anouk is a **famous** Dutch singer.

### 1976 - invoering [n] *implementation; introduction; launch*

De **invoering** van de wet loopt voorspoedig.
The **implementation** of the law is progressing well.

### 1977 - dossiers [n] *files*

Deze **dossiers** moeten vernietigd worden.
These **files** have to be destroyed.

### 1978 - broer [n] *brother*

Theo is jouw **broer**, toch?
Theo is your **brother**, right?

### 1979 - aanvankelijk [adj, adv] *initially*

**Aanvankelijk** was zijn studie makkelijk, maar later werd het moeilijk.

**Initially,** his course was easy, but later it got difficult.

### 1980 - mezelf [pron] *myself*

Ik zou graag meer tijd voor **mezelf** hebben.

I would like to have more time to **myself**.

### 1981 - openen [v] *to open (infinitive and plural subjects - present tense)*

We moeten de winkel binnen vijf minuten **openen**.

We have to **open** the shop within five minutes.

### 1982 - gewicht [n] *weight*

De baby had een gezond **gewicht**.

The baby had a healthy **weight**.

### 1983 - opvallend [adj, adv] *eye-catching(ly)*

De kleding van de circusartiesten was erg **opvallend**.

The clothes of the circus artists was very **eye-catching**.

### 1984 - verwachte [adj] *expected*

Het **verwachte** inkomen kwam niet.

The **expected** income didn't arrive.

### 1985 - bezoeken [n, v] *visits; to visit (infinitive and plural subjects - present tense)*

Hij gaat zijn grootouders morgen **bezoeken**.

He's going to **visit** his grandparents tomorrow.

### 1986 - interieur [n] *interior*

Uw kantoor heeft een prachtig **interieur**.

Your office has a beautiful **interior**.

### 1987 - enig [adj, pron] *cute, unique; only; some/any*

Heeft u **enig** idee hoe laat het is?
Do you have **any** idea what time it is?

### 1988 - verwerkt [v] *processed (past participle)*

We hebben het nieuws nog niet **verwerkt**.
We haven't **processed** the news yet.

### 1989 - recent [adj] *recent*

Onze scheiding is erg **recent**.
Our divorce is very **recent**.

### 1990 - herstel [n] *recovery; repair*

Succes met je **herstel**!
Good luck with your **recovery**!

### 1991 - goedkope [adj] *cheap*

Die **goedkope** pasta is goed genoeg.
That **cheap** pasta is good enough.

### 1992 - bewijs [n] *proof; to prove (1ˢᵗ and 2ⁿᵈ person - present tense)*

De juryleden vonden dat het **bewijs** niet genoeg was.
The jury members thought the **proof** was insufficient.

### 1993 - minimum [n] *minimum*

Dit bod is het **minimum**.
This offer is the **minimum**.

### 1994 - omvat [v] *to contain; to cover (singular subjects -*

*present tense)*

De les **omvat** de Romeinen in Nederland.
The lesson **covers** the Romans in The Netherlands.

### 1995 - gezelschap [n] *company*

Goed **gezelschap** en lekker eten, deze avond is perfect!
Good **company** and delicious food; this night is perfect!

### 1996 - negentig [num] *ninety*

**Negentig** euro voor die fiets, geweldige aanbieding!
**Ninety** euros for that bike, great offer!

### 1997 - talent [n] *talent*

Wat een **talent** heeft dat meisje!
What a **talent** that girl has!

### 1998 - compleet [adj, adv] *complete(ly)*

De schaakset is niet **compleet**.
The chess set isn't **complete**.

### 1999 - vis [n] *fish; to fish (1ˢᵗ and 2ⁿᵈ person - present tense)*

Er zitten omega-3-vetzuren in deze **vis**.
There are omega-3 fatty acids in this **fish**.

### 2000 - gelooft [v] *to believe (2ⁿᵈ and 3ʳᵈ person - present tense)*

Niemand **gelooft** het verhaaltje van het jongetje.
Nobody **believes** the boy's story.

# Conclusion

Well done! You've reached the very end of this wonderful list of the 2000 Most Common Words in Dutch! You can be proud of yourself: you've exposed yourself to the most common vocabulary, and if you've mastered these words, then you will have developed your understanding of non-fiction to 84%, your fiction to 86.1%, and your oral speech to 92.7%. Those are incredible numbers, considering how important the understanding of vocabulary is when learning a new language and using that to communicate in new languages and with different cultures.

We hope you've also learned a few interesting facts about The Netherlands and Belgium through the phrases presented here, since culture and language are so inextricably linked it's important not to separate the two.

If you feel you've made progress in Dutch, we're happy to have helped you and hope to see you again soon; we'll surely meet again in future books and learning material.

So, take care and study hard, and don't forget the tips we gave you at the beginning if you want to become a pro in Dutch:

- Set achievable goals
- Grab a study partner
- Practice the pronunciation out loud
- Make the phrases your own by changing some words

Lastly, if you liked the book, we would really appreciate a little review wherever you bought it.

PS: Keep an eye out for more books like this one; we have more material to help you learn and improve your Dutch! Head over to www.LingoMastery.com and read our free articles, sign up for our newsletter and check out our Youtube channel. We give away a lot of free stuff to accelerate your Dutch learning, and you don't want to miss that!

**THANKS FOR READING!**

Printed in Great Britain
by Amazon

79325455R00169